500 GREAT RAIL-TRAILS

A Directory of Multi-Use Paths Created from Abandoned Railroads

Julie A. Winterich
Karen-Lee Ryan

RAILS-TO-TRAILS CONSERVANCY

LIVING PLANET
PRESS

Los Angeles ● Washington, D.C.

Interior design and page layout: Mark Wood

Cover icons: Patricia Moritz

Four-panel cover design: Property of the
Rails-to-Trails Conservancy

**Discounts for bulk orders are available from the
publisher. Call 310-396-0188.**

Printed on recycled paper

ISBN 1-879326-20-5

Manufactured in the United States of America

10 9 8 7 6 5 4 3 2 1

ACKNOWLEDGEMENTS

The Rails-to-Trails Conservancy is very grateful to Tim Winterich for his assistance in updating the information and maps in this book. Many thanks also go to Michael Brilliot and Stewart Watkins for their help and also to RTC Chapter Coordinators Roger Storm, Ken Bryan, Tom Sexton, Terry Berrigan, Evan Kurrasch and Joe Ganem for compiling information for RTC's chapter states. Also, thanks to RTC Vice President Peter Harnik for his input.

Finally, special thanks to all the trail managers and Forest Service personnel listed in this directory who patiently responded to our detailed surveys and numerous phone calls, and who continue to provide leadership and direction to rail-trail projects across the country.

CONTENTS

HOW TO USE THIS BOOK

At the beginning of each state you will find a map showing the general location of each rail-trail listed in that state. The text description of each rail-trail includes the following information:

Trail Name

Endpoints: endpoints of the entire trail

Location: county(ies) and/or the name of the National Forest in which the trail is located

Length: length of the trail including how many miles are currently open and, for those trails that are built partially on abandoned corridors, the number of miles on abandoned rail line

Surface: the materials used to surface the trail

Contact: name, address, and phone number of each trail's manager

Most trail managers have maps or other descriptive brochures available free or for a small charge, and they can also answer specific questions about their trails. If a trail is not yet fully developed, the manager can provide information about which sections are presently open and usable.

LEGEND

In addition, each trail has a series of icons depicting uses allowed on the trail.

 walking, hiking and jogging

 fishing access

 bicycling

 cross-country skiing

 mountain bikes recommended

 snowmobiling

 horseback riding

ATVs

 wheelchair access

 trail within the National Forest System

in-line skating and roller-skating

Uses permitted on individual trails are based on trail surfaces and are determined solely by trail managers. The Rails-to-Trails Conservancy has no control over which uses are permitted and prohibited.

Wheelchair access is indicated for hard surface trails that are suitable for wheelchair users. All trails that allow bicycling also allow mountain bicycling but only on the trail surface, not in surrounding open areas. Trails that only list the mountain bicycling symbol have rougher terrains that are not suitable for road bikes. The all-terrain vehicle symbol does not include motorcycles and minibikes.

INTRODUCTION

Five-hundred rail-trails...five-hundred unique journeys.

The book you have in your hands will lead you to many diverse and exciting trail experiences such as bicycling through a three-quarter-mile railroad tunnel on Wisconsin's 32-mile Elroy Sparta Trail...or strolling along the historic waters of Virginia's New River Trail, the oldest river in North America. Explore the remains of once-thriving railroad communities by visiting the Ghost Town Trail in Pennsylvania...trace history along the Minuteman Trail outside Boston following the route marched by British soldiers during the Revolutionary War in 1776...or mountain bike along the sparkling Susan River against a backdrop of jagged canyon cliffs on Northern California's Bizz-Johnson Trail.

Whether you walk or use a wheelchair, bike or ride a horse, cross-country ski or enjoy snowmobiling, rail-trails are for you. Because they are built on abandoned railroad corridors, they offer gentle grades and easy access for all types of recreation enthusiasts. Echoing the once-thriving railroad system, rail-trails connect urban hubs to sprawling suburbs, traverse small towns and stretch through state and national forests.

Our changing railroad system spawned the rail-trail movement. In 1916, the United States boasted the largest rail system in the world with nearly 300,000 miles of steel connecting every large city and small town into a massive transportation network. Today, that impressive system has shrunk to less than 150,000 miles taking a back seat to cars, trucks and airplanes. As more than 2,000 miles of track are abandoned each year, unused corridors (with tracks and ties removed) offer a perfect backbone for another type of transportation network — and new recreation system — rail-trails.

The rail-trail movement began in the mid-1960s in the Midwest. In 1963, the late Chicago naturalist May Theilgaard Watts wrote a letter to the editor of the *Chicago Tribune* proposing constructive reuse of an abandoned right-of-way outside of the city. She wrote, "We are human beings. We are able to walk upright on two feet. We need a footpath. Right now there is a chance for Chicago and its suburbs to have a footpath, a long one." She evoked images of a trail rich in maple trees with stretches of prairie open to walkers and bicyclists. This practical letter inspired thousands of citizens to undertake the 20-year creation of the 55-mile Illinois Prairie Path, complete with hand-built bridges, prairie remnants and wildlife-rich wetlands.

The idea spread slowly. Wisconsin opened the Elroy-Sparta Trail in 1967. Seattle cut the ribbon on the Burke-Gilman in 1978. The first half of Virginia's W&OD came into service in 1981. In 1986, when the Rails-to-Trails Conservancy opened its doors and began helping communities see their dreams become reality, we knew of only

100 open rail-trails with an additional 90 projects underway. Today, 500 trails are open to the public for a total of more than 5,000 miles and more than 500 additional projects are in progress. While RTC does not promote the curtailment of railroad service or the abandonment of trackage, we work to keep abandoned rights-of-way in public ownership for trails. Also, rail-trails provide a means of preserving our nation's valuable corridor system for possible future rail use.

The invaluable benefits of rail-trails speak for themselves. When the Xenia-Yellow Springs trail opened in southern Ohio, wheelchair-bound Sandy Stonerock traveled to the local K-Mart on her own for the first time ever. An Iowa couple initially opposed a trail project that spanned the length of their farm but completely changed their outlook after the trail was built — and even opened a bed and breakfast for trail users. Overcome by Seattle's outraged citizens and banner headlines, a developer who bought a proposed extension of the Burke-Gilman Trail to build a dock for his boat, gave up his plans and signed the deed for the trail extension over to the community.

Every rail-trail has its own special features and this book was developed to help you discover and enjoy them all. We hope you will also help us. Please write to us about any new rail-trails you find, send us descriptions of your favorite including what you do and don't like, and suggest any changes we should include in our next edition. We count on users like you to keep us abreast of changes and new developments in the ever growing rail-trail movement.

If you enjoy rail-trails, join the movement to create more trails and save abandoned corridors from being lost forever. Even a small amount of time can help build more rail-trails.

- If you only have an hour, write a letter to your elected representative in favor of pro-rail-trail legislation, or to your local newspaper praising a trail or trail project, or to a friend — sharing the special qualities of rail-trails.
- If you have a day, volunteer to plant flowers or clean-up trash on a trail near you.
- If you have several hours a month, become an active member of a trail effort in your area.

Whatever your time commitment, get involved. The success of a community's rail-trail project depends on the level of its citizens' participation.

The ultimate goal of the Rails-to-Trails Conservancy is to help build an interconnected system of trails throughout the country. If you want to learn more about the rails-to-trails movement and help support the Conservancy, see the membership form in the back of this book.

Happy trails!

Julie Winterich
Rails-to-Trails Conservancy

ALABAMA

1 Chief Ladiga Trail

Endpoints: Maxwellborn to
Georgia state line
Location: Calhoun and
Cleburne Counties
Length: 3 miles to open in
Piedmont in early 1993 (will be
21 miles when completed)
Surface: Crushed stone

Contact:
Tommy Allison
City of Piedmont
P.O. Box 112
Piedmont, AL 36272
205-447-9007

2 Monte Sano Railway Trail

Endpoints: Bankhead Parkway
to Toll Gate Road
Location: Madison County
Length: 2 miles
Surface: Original ballast

Contact:
Rebecca Bergquist
Huntsville Land Trust
P.O. Box 43
Huntsville, AL 35804
205-534-5263

ARKANSAS

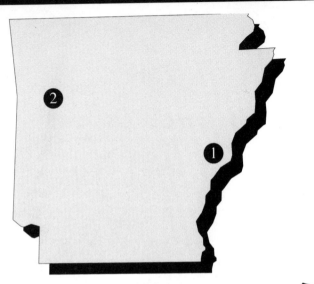

❶ *Marvell Bike Trail*

Endpoint: City of Marvell
Location: Phillips County
Length: 1.3 miles
Surface: Asphalt

Contact:
Ed Wallace, Mayor
City Hall
P.O. Box 837
Marvell, AR 72366
501-829-2573

❷ *Ozark Highlands Trail*

Endpoint: Ozark-St. Francis National Forest, milepost 25.8 to 37.0
Location: Franklin County
Length: 2.7 miles of 11.2-mile section is on abandoned rail line
Surface: Original ballast

Contact:
Joe Wallace
Recreation Staff Officer
Ozark-St. Francis National Forest
P.O. Box 1008
Russellville, AR 72801
501-968-2354

CALIFORNIA

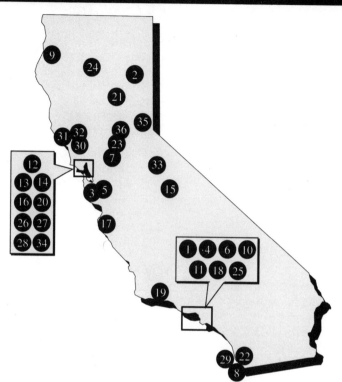

❶ *Alton Bike Trail*

Endpoints: Santa Ana
Location: Orange County
Length: 1.6 miles
Surface: Concrete

Contact:
City of Santa Ana
Recreation and Community
Services Agency
405 West 5th Street, 3rd Floor
P.O. Box 1988
Santa Ana, CA 92702
714-571-4200

❷ *Bizz Johnson Trail*

Endpoints: Susanville to
Westwood
Location: Lassen County
Length: 25 miles of 30-mile trail
is on abandoned rail line
Surface: Gravel and original
ballast

 on certain sections

(continued)

Contact:
Stan Bales
Bureau of Land Management
Eagle Lake Resource Area
2545 Riverside Drive
Susanville, CA 96130
916-257-0456

❸ Bol Park Bike Path

Endpoint: City of Palo Alto
Location: Santa Clara County
Length: 2 miles
Surface: Asphalt

Contact:
Julie Bonderant
Santa Clara County
Parks and Recreation
Trails and Pathways Committee
298 Garden Hill Drive
Los Gatos, CA 95030
408-358-3741

❹ Bud Turner Trail

Endpoint: City of Fullerton
Location: Orange County
Length: 3.8 miles
Surface: Dirt and chipped bark

Contact:
Gregg Meek
Community Services
Department
303 West Commonwealth
Avenue
Fullerton, CA 92632
714-738-6575

❺ Creek Trail

Endpoints: Alum Rock Park
Location: Santa Clara County
Length: 1.8 miles of 2.4-mile
trail is on abandoned rail line
Surface: Asphalt and dirt

Contact:
Dennis Mulgannon
Park Ranger
Alum Rock Park
16240 Alum Rock Avenue
San Jose, CA 95132
408-259-5477

❻ Duarte Bike Trail

Endpoints: City of Duarte
Location: Los Angeles County
Length: 1.5 miles
Surface: Asphalt with parallel
dirt treadway

Contact:
Donna Mitzel
City of Duarte
1600 Huntington Drive
Duarte, CA 91010
818-357-7931

7 Fairfield Linear Park

Endpoints: City of Fairfield
Location: Solano County
Length: 4 miles
Surface: Asphalt and concrete

Contact:
Gretchen Stranzl McCann
Fairfield Community Services
Department
1000 Webster Street
Fairfield, CA 94533
707-428-7431

8 Fay Avenue Bike Path

Endpoints: La Jolla
Location: San Diego County
Length: .75 miles
Surface: Asphalt

Contact:
Michael E. Jackson
Bicycle Coordinator
City of San Diego
1222 First Avenue
M.S. 503
San Diego, CA 92101
619-236-6064

9 Hammond Trail

Endpoint: McKinleyville
Location: Humboldt County
Length: 2.2 miles (will be 5 miles when completed)
Surface: Asphalt

Contact:
Karen Suiker
Business and Parks Manager
Humboldt County
Department of Public Works
1106 Second Street
Eureka, CA 95501
707-445-7652

10 Hermosa Valley Greenbelt

Endpoints: Hermosa Beach to Manhattan Beach
Location: Los Angeles County
Length: 2 miles
Surface: Wood chips

Contact:
Frederick R. Ferrin
City Manager
City of Hermosa Beach
Civic Center, 1315 Valley Drive
Hermosa Beach, CA 90254
310-318-0216

⓫ Juanita Cooke Greenbelt

Endpoint: City of Fullerton
Location: Orange County
Length: 1.3 miles
Surface: Wood chips

Contact:
Greg Meek
Community Services Dept.
303 West Commonwealth Avenue
Fullerton, CA 92632
714-738-6590

⓬ Lafayette/Moraga Trail

Endpoints: Lafayette to Moraga
Location: Contra Costa County
Length: 7.6 miles
Surface: Asphalt

Contact:
Steve Fiala, Trails Coordinator
East Bay Regional Park District
2950 Peralta Oaks Court
Oakland, CA 94605
510-635-0135

⓭ Lands End Trail

Endpoints: San Francisco
Location: San Francisco County
Length: 2 miles
Surface: Crushed stone

Contact:
Steve Prokop
Ocean District Ranger
Golden Gate National Recreation Area
Fort Mason Building 201
San Francisco, CA 94123
415-556-8371

⓮ Larkspur Path

Endpoints: City of Larkspur
Location: Marin County
Length: 1 mile
Surface: Asphalt

Contact:
Ron Miska, Assistant Open Space and Park Planner
Marin County Department of Parks, Open Space and Cultural Services
Marin Civic Center, Room 417
San Rafael, CA 94903
415-499-6387

⑮ Merced River Trail

Endpoints: El Portal, Gateway to the Yosemite National Park
Location: Mariposa County
Length: 8 miles
Surface: Original ballast

Contact:
Jim Eicher
Department of the Interior
Bureau of Land Management
63 Matoma Street
Folsom, CA 95630
916-985-4474

⑯ Mill Valley-Sausalito Path

Endpoints: Mill Valley to Sausalito
Location: Marin County
Length: 3.5 miles
Surface: Asphalt with parallel crushed stone treadways

Contact:
Ron Miska, Assistant Open Space and Park Planner
Marin County Department of Parks, Open Space and Cultural Services
Marin Civic Center, Room 417
San Rafael, CA 94903
415-499-6387

⑰ Monterey Peninsula Recreational Trail

Endpoints: Monterey to Pacific Grove
Location: Monterey County
Length: 4.3 miles
Surface: Cement with parallel dirt treadway

Monterey Section

Contact:
Kay Russo, Director
Monterey Recreation and Community Services
546 Dutra Street
Monterey, CA 93940
408-646-3866

Pacific Grove Section

Contact:
John Miller, Director
Pacific Grove Recreation Department
515 Gunipero Avenue
Pacific Grove, CA 93950
408-648-3130

18 Mt. Lowe Railroad Trail

Endpoints: Rubio Canyon to Mt. Lowe Trail Camp
Location: Los Angeles County
Length: 8 miles
Surface: Original ballast

Contact:
Oak Grove Ranger Section
Arroyo-Seco District
Oak Grove Park
Flint Ridge, CA 91011
818-790-1151

19 Ojai Valley Trail

Endpoints: Ventura to Ojai
Location: Ventura County
Length: 9.5 miles
Surface: Asphalt with parallel wood chip treadway

Contact:
Andrew Oshita, Parks Manager
GSA Parks
800 South Victoria
Ventura, CA 93009
805-654-3945

20 Old Railroad Grade

Endpoints: Mill Valley to Mt. Tamalpais State Park
Location: Marin County
Length: 9 miles
Surface: Original ballast

Contact:
Robert Badarocco
Lands Division Manager
Marin Municipal Water District
220 Nellen Avenue
Corte Madera, CA 94925
415-924-4600 Ext. 294

21 Paradise Memorial Trailway

Endpoints: Town of Paradise
Location: Butte County
Length: 5 miles
Surface: Asphalt and gravel

Contact:
Al McGreehan
Planning Director
Town of Paradise
Planning Office
5555 Skyway
Paradise, CA 95969
916-872-6284

㉒ Rose Canyon Bike Path

Endpoints: San Diego
Location: San Diego County
Length: 1.25 miles
Surface: Asphalt

Contact:
Michael E. Jackson
Bicycle Coordinator
City of San Diego
1222 First Avenue
M.S. 503
San Diego, CA 92101
619-236-6064

㉓ Sacramento Northern Bike Trail

Endpoints: Sacramento to Rio Linda
Location: Sacramento County
Length: 8 miles
Surface: Asphalt

Contact:
Kim Yee, Bikeway Coordinator
Transportation Division
1023 J Street
Sacramento, CA 95814
916-264-5145

㉔ Sacramento River Trail

Endpoints: Caldwell Park in Redding
Location: Shasta County
Length: 3 miles
Surface: Asphalt and original ballast

 on certain sections

Contact:
Terry Hanson
Associate Planner
City of Redding Planning Department
760 Park View
Redding, CA 96001
916-225-4030

㉕ Sally Pekarek Trail

Endpoints: City of Fullerton
Location: Orange County
Length: .25-mile of 1.75-mile trail is on abandoned rail line
Surface: Dirt

Contact:
Greg Meek, Director
Community Services Department
303 West Commonwealth Avenue
Fullerton, CA 92632
714-738-6590

26 San Ramon Valley Iron Horse Trail

Endpoints: Alamo to San Ramon
Location: Contra Costa County
Length: 9 miles developed from Alamo to Danville (will be 21 miles when completed)
Surface: Asphalt

Contact:
Steve Fiala, Trails Coordinator
East Bay Regional Park District
2950 Peralta Oaks Court
Oakland, CA 94605
510-635-0135

27 Sante Fe Greenway

Endpoints: Richmond to Berkeley
Location: Alameda and Contra Costa Counties
Length: 3.75 miles
Surface: Asphalt

Albany Section

Contact:
Jason Baker
Engineering Assistant
1000 San Pablo Avenue
Albany, CA 94706
510-528-5760

El Cerrito Section

Contact:
Joel Witherell
Manager of Community Services
10890 San Pablo
El Cerrito, CA 94530
510-215-4322

Berkeley Section

Contact:
Jeff Egeberg
Manager of Engineering
2180 Milvia Street
Berkeley, CA 94704
510-644-6540

28 Shepard Canyon Trail

Endpoints: City of Oakland
Location: Alameda County
Length: 1 mile of 3-mile trail is on abandoned rail line
Surface: Asphalt

Contact:
Martin Matarrese
Oakland Office of Parks and Recreation
3590 Sanborn Drive
Oakland, CA 94602
510-238-6326

㉙ Silver Strand Bikeway

Endpoints: Coronado to Imperial Beach
Location: San Diego County
Length: 7 miles
Surface: Asphalt

Contact:
G.L. Andy Anderson, Director
Public Services Department
City of Coronado
1300 First Street
Coronado, CA 92118-1595
619-522-7380

㉚ Sir Francis Drake Bikeway Improvement

Endpoints: Samuel P. Taylor State Park to Tocaloma
Location: Marin County
Length: 5 miles
Surface: Asphalt, hard-packed dirt and gravel

Contact:
Lanny Waggoner
State Park Ranger
Samuel P. Taylor State Park
P.O. Box 251
Lagunitas, CA 94938
415-488-9897

㉛ Sonoma Bike Path

Endpoints: City of Sonoma
Location: Sonoma County
Length: 1.5 miles
Surface: Asphalt

Contact:
Patricia Wagner
City of Sonoma
#1 The Plaza
Sonoma, CA 95476
707-938-3743

㉜ Sonoma County Bike Trail

Endpoints: Santa Rosa to Forestville
Location: Sonoma County
Length: 3 miles (will be 10 miles when completed)
Surface: Asphalt

Contact:
Philip Sales
Sonoma County Regional Parks
410 Fiscal Drive
Santa Rosa, CA 95403
707-527-2041

33 Sugarpine Railway Trail

Endpoints: Twain Harte
Location: Tuolumne County
Length: 9 miles
Surface: Dirt and gravel

 on certain sections

Contact:
Mike Cook
Recreation Technician
Mi-Wok Ranger District
P.O. Box 100
Mi-Wuk Village, CA 95346
209-586-3234

34 Tiburon Linear Park

Endpoints: Blackie's Pasture to Belvedere
Location: Marin County
Length: 2.3 miles
Surface: Asphalt

Contact:
Ron Miska, Assistant Open Space and Park Planner
Marin County Department of Parks, Open Space and Cultural Services
Marin Civic Center, Room 417
San Rafael, CA 94903
415-499-6387

35 Truckee River Bike Trail

Endpoints: Tahoe City
Location: Placer County
Length: 4 miles
Surface: Asphalt

Contact:
Sandy Coambs, Director
Department of Parks and Recreation
Tahoe City P.U.D.
P.O. Box 33
Tahoe City, CA 95730
916-538-3796

36 Western States Pioneer Express Recreation Trail

Endpoints: Auburn to Squaw Valley
Location: Placer County
Length: 2 miles of 100-mile trail is on abandoned rail line
Surface: Dirt and gravel

Contact:
Mike Vanhook
Supervising Ranger
California Department of Parks and Recreation
P.O. Box 3266
Auburn, CA 95604
916-885-4527

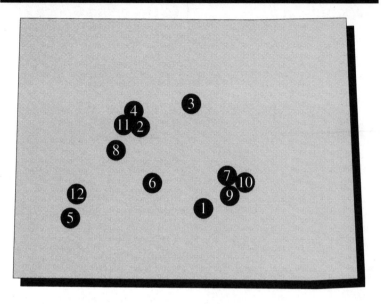

❶ *Arkansas Riverwalk Trail*

Endpoints: Canon City
Location: Fremont County
Length: 2.5 miles of 3.5-mile trail is on abandoned rail line
Surface: Crushed stone

 on certain sections

Contact:
Jeff Friesner, Manager
Canon City Metropolitan
Recreation and Park District
306 North Sixteenth Street
Suite I
Canon City, CO 81212
719-275-1578

❷ *Blue River Recreation Trail*

Endpoints: Breckenridge to Dillon Reservoir at Farmer's Corner
Location: Summit County
Length: 3 miles of 6-mile trail is on abandoned rail line
Surface: Asphalt

Contact:
Scott Hobson
Recreation Planner
Summit County Government
P.O. Box 68
Breckenridge, CO 80424
303-453-2561

❸ Fowler Trail

Endpoints: Eldorado Canyon
State Park, Eldorado Springs
Location: Boulder County
Length: .25 mile
Surface: Crushed stone

Contact:
Bob Toll
Park Manager
Eldorado Canyon State Park
P.O. Box B
Eldorado Springs, CO 80025
303-494-3943

❹ Frisco-Farmer's Corner Recreation Trail

Endpoints: Frisco to Dillon
Reservoir at Farmer's Corner
Location: Summit County
Length: 3 miles of 3.5-mile trail
is on abandoned rail line
Surface: Asphalt

Contact:
Scott Hobson
Recreation Planner
Summit County Government
P.O. Box 68
Breckenridge, CO 80424
303-453-2561

❺ Galloping Goose Trail

Endpoints: Telluride
Location: San Miguel County
Length: 4 miles (will be 21 miles
when completed)
Surface: Original ballast

 on certain sections

Contact:
Bill Dunkleberger
Forestry Technician
U.S. Forest Service
P.O. Box 695
Ophir, CO 81426
303-728-4211

❻ Midland Bike Trail

Endpoints: Pike and San Isabel
National Forest, Buena Vista to
Trout Creek Pass
Location: Chaffee County
Length: 12 miles
Surface: Original ballast

Contact:
Carrie Sarber
Outdoor Recreation Planner
Salida Ranger District
325 W. Rainbow Blvd.
Salida, CO 81201
719-539-3591

❼ New Santa Fe Regional Trail

Endpoints: Palmer Lake to Colorado Springs
Location: El Paso County
Length: 10 miles of 15-mile trail is on abandoned rail line
Surface: Rolled gravel

 on certain sections

Contact:
Mickey Carter, Director
El Paso County Park Department
2002 Creek Crossing
Colorado Springs, CO 80906
719-520-6375

❽ Rio Grande Trail

Endpoints: City of Aspen
Location: Pitkin County
Length: 7.5 miles
Surface: Asphalt and dirt

 on certain sections

Contact:
Patrick Duffield
Trails Supervisor
Parks Department
City of Aspen
130 South Galena
Aspen, CO 81611
303-920-5120

❾ Rock Island Trail

Endpoints: Colorado Springs
Location: El Paso County
Length: 2.7 miles
Surface: Recycled asphalt

Contact:
Craig R. Blewitt, Senior Planner
Colorado Springs
Comprehensive Planning Division
P.O. Box 1575, Mail Code 311
Colorado Springs, CO 80901
719-578-6692

❿ Shooks Run Trail

Endpoints: Colorado Springs
Location: El Paso County
Length: 1.8 miles
Surface: Asphalt and concrete

Contact:
Craig Blewitt, Senior Planner
Colorado Springs
Comprehensive Planning Division
P.O. Box 1575, Mail Code 311
Colorado Springs, CO 80901
719-578-6692

⓫ Ten Mile Canyon Recreation Trail

Endpoints: Frisco to Vail
Location: Summit and Eagle Counties
Length: 6 miles of 24-mile trail is on abandoned rail line
Surface: Asphalt

Summit County Section

Contact:
Scott Hobson
Recreation Planner
Summit County Government
P.O. Box 68
Breckenridge, CO 80424
303-453-2561

Eagle County Section

Contact:
Keith Montage, Planner
Eagle County Community
Development
P.O. Box 179
Eagle, CO 81631
303-328-8730

⓬ Uncompahgre River Trail Bikepath

Endpoints: City of Montrose
Location: Montrose County
Length: 5 miles
Surface: Concrete

Contact:
Dennis Erickson
Parks Superintendent
City of Montrose
P.O. Box 790
Montrose, CO 81402
303-249-4534

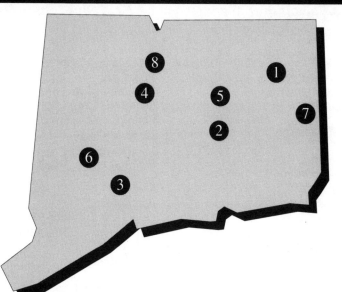

CONNECTICUT

① *Airline State Park Trail (Northern Section)*

Endpoints: Windham to Putnam
Location: Windham County
Length: 26.8 miles
Surface: Gravel and original ballast

Contact:
John Folsom
Mashamoquet Brook State Park
Pomfret Center, CT 06259
203-928-6121

② *Airline State Park Trail (Southern Section)*

Endpoints: Windham to East Hampton
Location: Windham, New London, Middlesex and Hartford Counties
Length: 22.7 miles
Surface: Gravel and original ballast

Contact:
Joe Hickey
Bureau of Outdoor Recreation
Department of Environmental Protection
165 Capital Avenue
Hartford, CT 06106
203-566-2304

❸ Farmington Canal Line State Park Trail

Endpoints: Cheshire to Hamden
Location: New Haven County
Length: 6.8 miles
Surface: Gravel and dirt

Contact:
Dick Bartlem
Cheshire Department of Parks
and Recreation
559 S. Main St.
Cheshire, CT 06410
203-272-2743

❹ Farmington River Fishing Access Area

Endpoints: Farmington to
Collinsville
Location: Hartford County
Length: 3.5 miles
Surface: Crushed stone

Contact:
Daniel Dickinson, Park and
Recreation Supervisor
Farmington Headquarters
178 Scott Swamp Road
Farmington, CT 06032
203-677-1819

❺ Hop River State Park Trail

Endpoints: Manchester to
Windham
Location: Hartford, Toland and
Windham Counties
Length: 19.6 miles
Surface: Gravel

Contact:
Joe Hickey
Bureau of Outdoor Recreation
Department of Environmental
Protection
165 Capital Ave.
Hartford, CT 06106
203-566-2304

❻ Larkin Bridle Trail

Endpoints: Southbury to
Waterbury
Location: New Haven County
Length: 10.7 miles
Surface: Original ballast and
cinders

Contact:
Tim O'Donoghue, Supervisor
Southford Falls State Park
Quaker Farms Road, Route 188
Southbury, CT 06488
203-264-5169

❼ Moosup Valley State Park Trail

Endpoints: Village of Moosup to Rhode Island border
Location: Windham County
Length: 8.1 miles
Surface: Gravel and original ballast

Contact:
Mike Reid
Park and Recreation Supervisor
Pachaug State Forest
Headquarters
P.O. Box 5
Voluntown, CT 06384
203-346-2920

❽ Stratton Brook Park/ Town Forest Trail

Endpoints: Stratton Brook State Park to Simsbury
Location: Hartford County
Length: 2.5 miles
Surface: Crushed stone

Stratton Brook Section

Contact:
Dan Dickinson, Supervisor
Stratton Brook State Park
194 Stratton Brook Road
Simsbury, CT 06070
203-242-1158

Town Forest Section

Contact:
Gerald G. Toner, Director
Department of Culture, Parks and Recreation
933 Hopmeadow Street
Simsbury, CT 06070
203-651-3751

❶ *Boca Grande Bike Path*

Endpoints: Gasparilla Island
Location: Lee County
Length: 6.5 miles
Surface: Asphalt

Contact:
Bicycle Coordinator
Lee County Department of
Transportation
2022 Hendry Street
Fort Myers, FL 33901
813-335-2220

❷ *Cady Way to Fashion Square Greenway*

Endpoints: Cady Way to
Fashion Square
Location: Orange County
Length: 2 miles (will be 4 miles
when completed)
Surface: Concrete and asphalt

Contact:
Mrs. Pat Hopkins
City of Orlando
1414 N. Orange Avenue
Orlando, FL 32804
407-246-2011

❸ Gainesville-Hawthorne State Trail

Endpoints: Gainesville to Hawthorne
Location: Alachua County
Length: 14 miles
Surface: Crushed limestone

Contact:
Jack Gillen, Park Manager
Paynes Prairie State Preserve
Route 2, Box 41
Micanopy, FL 32667
904-466-3397

❹ General James A. Van Fleet State Trail

Endpoints: Polk City to Mabel
Location: Sumter, Polk and Lake Counties
Length: 28.5 miles
Surface: Dirt and gravel

Contact:
Robert Seifer, Park Programs Development Specialist
Division of Parks and Recreation
Florida Department of Natural Resources
12549 State Park Drive
Clermont, FL 34711
904-394-2280

❺ Pinellas Trail

Endpoints: St. Petersburg to Tarpon Springs
Location: Pinellas County
Length: 22 miles developed between Seminole and Tarpon Springs (will be 47 miles when completed with 36 miles on abandoned rail line)
Surface: Asphalt

Contact:
Jerry Cummings
Pinellas Trail Park Ranger
Pinellas County Parks Department
631 Chestnut Street
Clearwater, FL 34616
813-581-2953

❻ South Depot Avenue Bike Route

Endpoints: Gainesville
Location: Alachua County
Length: 1 mile
Surface: Dirt and gravel

Contact:
Bicycle Coordinator
Traffic and Engineering Department
Mail Station 28
P.O. Box 490
Gainesville, FL 32602
904-334-2130

❼ Tallahassee - St. Marks Historic Railroad State Trail

Endpoints: Tallahassee to St. Marks
Location: Leon and Wakulla Counties
Length: 16 miles
Surface: Asphalt with parallel dirt treadway

Contact:
Clifton Maxwell, Trail Manager
Division of Parks and Recreation
Florida Department of Natural Resources
1022 Desoto Park Drive
Tallahassee, FL 32301
904-922-6007

❽ Waldo Road Trail

Endpoints: Gainesville
Location: Alachua County
Length: 3 miles
Surface: Asphalt

Contact:
Bicycle Coordinator
Traffic and Engineering Department
Mail Station 28
P.O. Box 490
Gainesville, FL 32602
904-334-2107

❾ Withlacoochee State Trail

Endpoints: Trilby to south of Gulf Junction
Location: Citrus, Pasco and Hernando Counties
Length: 11 miles developed between Brooksville and Istachatta (will be 47 miles when completed)
Surface: Gravel and dirt

Contact:
Robert Seifer, Park Programs Development Specialist
Division of Parks and Recreation
Florida Department of Natural Resources
12549 State Park Drive
Clermont, FL 34711
904-394-2280

GEORGIA

❶ *Chatahoochee Trail*

Endpoints: Columbus
Location: Muscogee County
Length: 1 mile (will be 11.5 miles when completed)
Surface: Asphalt

Contact:
Rick Gordon, Director
Columbus Parks and
Recreation Department
P.O. Box 1340
Columbus, GA 31993
404-571-4785

❷ *Heritage Park Trail*

Endpoints: Town of Rome
Location: Floyd County
Length: 1.5 miles
Surface: Asphalt

Contact:
Tim Banks, Assistant Director
Rome-Floyd County Parks and
Recreation Authority
300 West Third Street
Rome, GA 30165
706-291-0766

❸ McQueen Island Historic Scenic Multipurpose Trail

Endpoints: McQueen Island
Location: Chatham County
Length: 3 miles (will be 6 miles when completed)
Surface: Crushed limestone

Contact:
Jim Golden, Director
Chatham County Parks,
Recreation and Cultural Affairs
Department
P.O. Box 1746
Savannah, GA 31402
912-352-0032

❹ The G.R.I.T.S. Trail

Endpoints: Atlanta to Alabama state line
Location: Cobb, Paulding and Polk Counties
Length: 35 miles
Surface: Crushed stone
The first section is scheduled to open in early 1993

Contact:
Gary Jenkins, President
Georgia Rails Into Trails Society
P.O. Box 371
Lithia Springs, GA 30057
404-920-2881

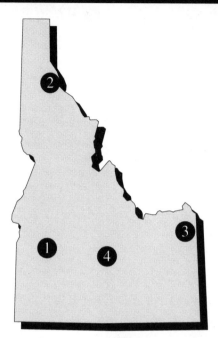

❶ *Greenbelt Trail*

Endpoints: Lucky Peak
Reservoir to Boise
Location: Ada County
Length: 2 miles of 18-mile trail
is on abandoned rail line
Surface: Asphalt

Contact:
Jack Logan
Ada County Parks
and Recreation
650 Main Street
Boise, ID 83702
208-343-1328

❷ *Mullan Pass - Lookout Pass Loop*

Endpoints: Idaho Panhandle
National Forest, Shoshone Park
Picnic Area to Lookout Pass
(Montana state line)
Location: Shoshone County
Length: 8 miles
Surface: Original ballast

Contact:
Bill Cook, Recreation Officer
Idaho Panhandle National
Forest
P.O. Box 14
Silverton, ID 83867
208-752-1221

❸ Yellowstone Branch Line Trail

Endpoints: Warm River to Montana state line
Location: Fremont County Targhee National Forest
Length: 34 miles
Surface: Original ballast

 on certain sections

Contacts:
Bart Andreasen
or Marian Boulter
Targhee National Forest
P.O. Box 208
St. Anthony, ID 83445
208-624-3151

❹ Wood River Trails

Endpoints: Ketchum to Bellevue
Location: Blaine County
Length: 20 miles
Surface: Asphalt

Contact:
Mary Austin Crofts, Director
Blaine County Recreation
District
P.O. Box 297
Hailey, ID 83333
208-788-2117

ILLINOIS

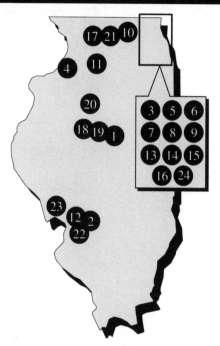

❶ Constitution Trail

Endpoints: Bloomington to Normal
Location: McLean County
Length: 4.3 miles (will be 5.3 miles when completed)
Surface: Asphalt

Contact:
Keith Rich, Director
Bloomington Parks and Recreation Department
109 East Olive Street
Bloomington, IL 61701
309-823-4260

❷ Delyte Morris Bikeway

Endpoints: Edwardsville
Location: Madison County
Length: 2.6 miles
Surface: Asphalt and crushed stone

Contact:
Anna Schonlau
Assistant Recreation Director
Recreation Department
Southern Illinois University at Edwardsville
P.O. Box 1057
Edwardsville, IL 62026
618-692-3235

27

❸ *Fox River Trail*

Endpoints: Algonquin to Aurora
Location: Kane County
Length: 33 miles
Surface: Asphalt

Contacts:
Jon Duerr, Superintendent
Kane County Forest Preserve
719 Batavia Avenue
Geneva, IL 60134
708-232-5981

Charles E. Hoscheit, Director
Fox Valley Park District
712 South River Street
Aurora, IL 60506
708-897-0516

❹ *Great River Trail*

Endpoints: Rock Island to
Savanna
Location: Carroll, Rock Island
and Whiteside Counties
Length: 27 miles developed
between Moline and Hampton
and between Albany and Fulton
(will be 65 miles when
completed)
Surface: Asphalt, concrete and
crushed stone

 on certain sections

Contact:
Patrick Marsh
Bi-State Regional Commission
1504 Third Avenue
Rock Island, IL 61201
309-793-6300

❺ *Great Western Trail*

Endpoints: St. Charles to
Sycamore
Location: Kane and DeKalb
Counties
Length: 18 miles
Surface: Asphalt and crushed
stone

 on certain sections

Contacts:
Jon Duerr, Superintendent
Kane County Forest Preserve
719 Batavia Avenue
Geneva, IL 60134
708-232-5981

Terry Hannan, Superintendent
Dekalb County Forest Preserve
110 E. Sycamore Street
Sycamore, IL 60178
815-895-7191

❻ Great Western Trail
(DuPage Parkway Section)

Endpoints: Villa Park to West Chicago
Location: DuPage County
Length: 12 miles
Surface: Crushed limestone

 on certain sections

Contact:
Charles Tokarski
Chief of Traffic Planning and Programming
DuPage County Division of Transportation
130 N. County Farm Road
Wheaton, IL 60189
708-682-7318

❼ Green Bay Trail

Endpoints: Highland Park to Wilmette
Location: Lake and Cook Counties
Length: 9.5 miles
Surface: Asphalt and crushed stone

Highland Park Section

Contact:
Larry King, Superintendent
Highland Park Forestry Department
1150 Half Day Road
Highland Park, IL 60035
708-432-0800 ext. 282

Glencoe Section

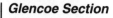

Contact:
John Houde
Village of Glencoe
675 Village Court
Glencoe, IL 60022
708-835-4111

Winnetka Section

Contact:
Dan Newport, Director
Winnetka Park District
510 Green Bay Road
Winnetka, IL 60093
708-501-2040

Wilmette Section

Contact:
Bill Lambrecht
Wilmette Park District
1200 Wilmette Avenue
Wilmette, IL 60091
708-256-6100

⑧ Illinois Prairie Path

Endpoints: Maywood to Wheaton with spurs to Aurora, Batavia, Geneva and Elgin
Location: Cook, DuPage and Kane Counties
Length: 50 miles
Surface: Asphalt, crushed stone and dirt

 on certain sections

Contacts:
Jean Mooring
Illinois Prairie Path, Inc.
P.O. Box 1086
Wheaton, IL 60189
708-665-5310

Charles Tokarski
DuPage County Division of Transportation
130 North County Farm Road
Wheaton, IL 60187
708-682-7318

Charles E. Hoscheit, Director
Fox Valley Park District
P.O. Box 818
Aurora, IL 60507
708-897-0516

⑨ Libertyville Trail

Endpoints: Libertyville
Location: Lake County
Length: 3 miles
Surface: Crushed stone

Contact:
Steve Magmusen
Director of Public Works
200 East Cook Avenue
Libertyville, IL 60048
708-362-2430

⑩ Long Prairie Trail

Endpoints: Poplar Grove to McHenry County Line
Location: Boone County
Length: 6.5 miles
Surface: Asphalt

Contact:
Boone County Conservation District
7600 Appleton Road
Belvidere, IL 61008
815-547-7935

🕚 Lowell Parkway Bicycle Path

Endpoints: Dixon
Location: Lee County
Length: 3 miles
Surface: Original ballast and gravel (will be asphalt when completed)

Contact:
Dave Zinnen
Director of Administration and Recreation
Debra Carey, Naturalist
Dixon Park District
804 Palmyra Avenue
Dixon, IL 61021
815-284-3306

🕛 Madison County Nature Trail

Endpoints: Edwardsville
Location: Madison County
Length: 3 miles developed from Edwardsville to Southern Illinois University (will be 6.3 miles when completed)
Surface: Crushed stone

Contact:
George Arnold
Madison County Trail Volunteers
1306 St. Louis Street
Edwardsville, IL 62025
618-656-3994

🕐 McHenry County Prairie Trail (North)

Endpoints: Ringwood to Wisconsin line north of Richmond
Location: McHenry County
Length: 7.5 miles
Surface: Original ballast

Contact:
Steve Weller
Executive Director
McHenry County Conservation District
6512 Harts Road
Ringwood, IL 60072
815-678-4431

🕑 McHenry County Prairie Trail (South)

Endpoints: Crystal Lake to Kane County line
Location: McHenry County
Length: 4.5 miles
Surface: Asphalt

Contact:
Steve Weller
Executive Director
McHenry County Conservation District
6512 Harts Road
Ringwood, IL 60072
815-678-4431

⑮ North Shore Bike Trail

Endpoints: Lake Bluff to Wisconsin state line
Location: Lake County
Length: 14 (will be 14.7 miles when completed)
Surface: Limestone screenings

Contact:
Martin G. Buehler
Director of Transportation
Lake County Division
of Transportation
600 W. Winchester Road
Libertyville, IL 60048
708-362-3950

⑯ Palatine Trail

Endpoints: Palatine to Rolling Meadows
Location: Cook County
Length: 1 mile of 28-mile trail is on abandoned rail line
Surface: Asphalt

Contact:
Fred P. Hall
Director of Parks and
Recreation
Palatine Park District
250 E. Wood Street
Palatine, IL 60067
708-991-0333

⑰ Pecatonica Prairie Path

Endpoints: Rockford to Freeport
Location: Stephenson and Winnebago Counties
Length: 21 miles
Surface: Original ballast

 on certain sections

Contacts:
David Derwent, President
Pecatonica Prairie Path, Inc.
Box 354
Pecatonica, IL 61063
815-235-2103

Mary Mohaupt
Pectonica Prairie Path, Inc.
Box 354
Pecatonica, IL 61063
815-239-2180

⑱ Pimiteoui Bike Trail

Endpoints: Peoria
Location: Peoria County
Length: 2 miles
Surface: Asphalt

Contacts:
Carol Hallock, President
Pimiteoui Trail Association
3016 N. Western Avenue
Peoria, IL 61604
309-688-1165

George M. Burrier
213 N. Oklahoma Avenue
Morton, IL 61550
309-266-5085

⑲ River Trail of Illinois

Endpoints: East Peoria to Morton
Location: Tazwell County
Length: 5.3 miles developed in East Peoria (will be 9 miles when completed)
Surface: Asphalt

Contact:
Jim Coutts, Director
Fon du Lac Park District
201 Veterans Drive
East Peoria, IL 61611
309-699-3923

⑳ Rock Island Trail State Park

Endpoints: Pioneer Parkway to Toulon
Location: Peoria and Stark Counties
Length: 28 miles
Surface: Crushed limestone

Contacts:
Paul Oltman, Trail Ranger
Rock Island Trail State Park
P.O. Box 64
Wyoming, IL 61491
309-695-2228

George M. Barrier
213 N. Oklahoma Avenue
Morton, IL 61550
309-266-5085

㉑ Rock River Recreation Path

Endpoints: Rockford to Love's Park
Location: Winnebago County
Length: 3.3 miles
Surface: Asphalt

Contact:
Vance Barrie
Marketing Coordinator
Rockford Park District
1401 North Second Street
Rockford, IL 61107-3086
815-987-8694

㉒ Ronald J. Foster Heritage Trail

Endpoints: Glen Carbon
Location: Madison County
Length: 3.2 miles
Surface: Asphalt

Contact:
Glen Carbon Village Hall
P.O. Box 757
Glen Carbon, IL 62034
618-288-1200

㉓Sam Vadalabene Bike Trail

Endpoints: Alton to Grafton
Location: Madison and Jersey Counties
Length: 3.5 miles of 14.2-mile trail is on abandoned rail line
Surface: Asphalt

Contact:
Ron Tedesco
Illinois Department
of Transportation
1100 Eastport Plaza Drive
P.O. Box 988
Collinsville, IL 62234-6198
618-346-3100

㉔Virgil Gilman Nature Trail

Endpoints: Sugar Grove to Aurora
Location: Kane County
Length: 12 miles
Surface: Asphalt and crushed stone

on certain sections

Contact:
Charles E. Hoscheit, Director
Fox Valley Park District
P.O. Box 818
Aurora, IL 60507
708-897-0516

INDIANA

❶ Auburn to Waterloo Bike Trail

Endpoints: Auburn to Waterloo
Location: Dekalb County
Length: 4 miles
Surface: Cement

Contact:
Andy Jagoda
Parks and Recreation
Superintendent
Auburn Parks Department
P.O. Box 506
Auburn, IN 46706
219-925-8245

❷ Bloomington Rail Trail Project

Endpoints: Bloomington to Victor
Location: Monroe County
Length: 4 miles (will be 6.2 miles when completed)
Surface: Original ballast

Contact:
Leslie Clark
Bloomington Parks
and Recreation Department
349 S. Walnut Street
Bloomington, IN 47401
812-332-9668

35

❸ East Bank Trail

Endpoints: South Bend
Location: St. Joseph County
Length: .5 mile
Surface: Asphalt

Contact:
Karl Stevens
South Bend Parks Department
301 S. St. Louis Boulevard
South Bend, IN 46617
219-284-9401

❹ Erie Trail Linear Park

Endpoints: Hammond
Location: Lake County
Length: 3.75 miles
Surface: Asphalt

Contact:
Donald E. Thomas
City Planner
Department of Planning
City of Hammond
649 Conkey
Hammond, IN 46324
219-853-6398

❺ Prairie-Duneland Trail

Endpoints: Portage City
Location: Porter County
Length: 1.5 miles (will be 6 miles when completed)
Surface: Asphalt

Contact:
Carl Fisher, Superintendent
Portage Parks and Recreation
Department
2100 Willowcreek Road
Portage, IN 46368
219-762-1675

❻ Whitewater Canal Trail

Endpoints: Metamora to Brookville
Location: Franklin County
Length: 2 miles (will be 8 miles when completed)
Surface: Dirt

Contact:
Mike Martin
Streams and Trails Specialist
Indiana Department of Natural Resources
402 West Washington
Room 271
Indianapolis, IN 46204
317-232-4070

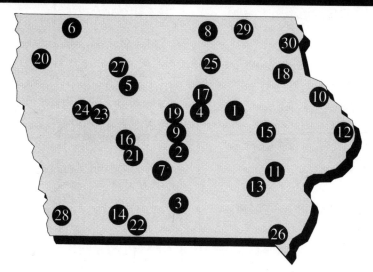

IOWA

❶ Cedar Valley Nature Trail

Endpoints: Hiawatha to Evansdale
Location: Linn, Benton, Buchanan and Black Hawk Counties
Length: 52 miles (.5 miles temporarily closed north of Urbana)
Surface: Crushed stone

Linn and Benton County Section

Contact:
Dan Biechler, Director
Linn County Conservation Board
1890 County Home Road
Marion, IA 52302
319-398-3505

Buchanan and Black Hawk County Section

Contact:
Steve Finegan, Executive Director, or Bert Hallewas
Black Hawk County Conservation Board
2410 West Lone Tree Road
Cedar Falls, IA 50613
319-277-1536

❷ Chichaqua Valley Trail

Endpoints: Bondurant to Baxter
Location: Polk and Jasper Counties
Length: 21 miles
Surface: Crushed stone

 on certain sections

Jasper County Section

Contact:
John C. Parsons, Parks Officer
Jasper County Conservation Board
115 North Second Ave., East-Newton, IA 50208
515-792-9780

Polk County Section

Contact:
Bob Hamilton, Director
Polk County Conservation Board
Jester Park
Granger, IA 50109
515-999-2557

❸ Cinder Path

Endpoints: Chariton to County line
Location: Lucas County
Length: 13 miles
Surface: Original ballast

Contact:
Dwayne Clanin, Supervisor
P.O. Box 78
Chariton, IA 50049
515-774-2314

❹ Comet Trail

Endpoints: Conrad to east of Beaman
Location: Grundy County
Length: 4 miles (will be 6.3 miles when completed)
Surface: Crushed limestone

on undeveloped section

Contact:
Samuel K. Gooden, Director
Grundy County Conservation Board
P.O. Box 36
Morrison, IA 50657
319-345-2688

❺ Fort Dodge Nature Trail

Endpoints: Fort Dodge
Location: Webster County
Length: 3 miles
Surface: Crushed stone

Contact:
Michael R. Norris, City Forester
Department of Parks,
Recreation and Forestry
813 First Avenue South
Fort Dodge, IA 50501
515-573-5791

❻ Great Lakes Spine Trail

Endpoints: Milford to Spirit Lake
Location: Dickinson County
Length: 10 miles
Surface: Asphalt

on certain sections only

Contact:
John J. Walters, Director
Dickinson County Conservation Board
1013 Okoboji Avenue
Milford, IA 51351
712-338-4786

❼ Great Western Trail

Endpoints: Des Moines to Martensdale
Location: Polk and Warren Counties
Length: 18.2 miles
Surface: Crushed limestone and asphalt

on certain sections

Polk County Section

Contact:
Bob Hamilton, Director
Polk County Conservation Board
Jester Park
Granger, IA 50109
515-999-2557

Warren County Section

Contact:
Jim Priebe, Director
Warren County Conservation Board
1565 118th Avenue
Indianola, IA 50125
515-961-6169

⑧ Harry Cook Nature Trail

Endpoints: Osage to Spring Park
Location: Mitchell County
Length: 2 miles
Surface: Crushed limestone

on certain sections

Contact:
Ted Funk, Director
Parks and Recreation Dept.
Osage, IA 50461
515-732-3709

⑨ Heart of Iowa Trail

Endpoints: Melbourne to Slater
Location: Story and Marshall Counties
Length: 32 miles
Surface: Crushed limestone and original ballast

Contact:
Steve Lekwa, Deputy Director
Story County Conservation Board
Hickory Grove Park
Colo, IA 50056
515-377-2229

⑩ Heritage Trail

Endpoints: Dubuque to Dyersville
Location: Dubuque County
Length: 26 miles
Surface: Crushed limestone

 on certain sections

Contact:
Bob Walton, Executive Director
Dubuque County Conservation Board
Swiss Valley Nature Center
13768 Swiss Valley Road
Peosta, IA 52068
319-556-6745

⑪ Hoover Nature Trail

Endpoints: Cedar Rapids to Burlington
Location: Cedar, Johnson, Muscatine, Louisa and Des Moines Counties
Length: 23 miles in four sections (will be 115 miles when completed)
Surface: Crushed limestone and original ballast

 on certain sections

Contact:
Milly Gregg
Hoover Nature Trail, Inc.
Box 123
West Liberty, IA 52776
319-627-2626

⑫ Jackson County Trail

Endpoints: Spragueville to County Road Z34
Location: Jackson County
Length: 3.8 miles
Surface: Crushed stone and original ballast

Contact:
Ann Burns
Jackson County Conservation Board
Courthouse
Maquoketa, IA 52060
319-652-3783

⑬ Kewash Trail

Endpoints: Keota to Washington
Location: Washington County
Length: 14.8 miles
Surface: Crushed limestone

Contact:
Kathy Cuddeback
Washington County Conservation Board
Courthouse
Box 889
Washington, IA 52353
319-653-7765

⑭ Maple Leaf Pathway

Endpoints: Diagonal
Location: Ringgold County
Length: 2.5 miles
Surface: Crushed stone

Contact:
Rick Hawkins, Director
Ringgold County Conservation Board
Box 83A, RR 1
Mt. Ayr, IA 50854
515-464-2787

⑮ Old Interurban Trail

Endpoints: Cedar Rapids to Mt. Vernon
Location: Linn County
Length: 3.8 miles
Surface: Original ballast

Contact:
Patty Lee
930 44th Street, S.E.
Cedar Rapids, IA 52403
319-363-6212

⑯ Perry to Rippey Trail

Endpoints: Perry to Rippey
Location: Greene, Dallas and Boone Counties
Length: 9 miles
Surface: Original ballast and dirt

Greene County Section

Contact:
Dan Towers, Director
Greene County Conservation Board
Courthouse
Jefferson, IA 50129
515-386-4629

Dallas County Section

Contact:
Jeff Logsdon, Director
Dallas County Conservation Board
1477 K Avenue
Perry, IA 50220
515-465-3577

Boone County Section

Contact:
Tom Foster, Director
Boone County Conservation Board
610 H Avenue
Ogden, IA 50212
515-353-4237

⑰ Pioneer Trail

Endpoints: Reinbeck to Holland
Location: Grundy County
Length: 9 miles developed near Morrison and from Grundy Center to Holland (will be 12 miles when completed, 9 miles on abandoned rail line)
Surface: Crushed stone with parallel grass treadway

Contact:
Samuel K. Gooden, Director
Grundy County Conservation Board
P.O. Box 36
Morrison, IA 50657
319-345-2688

⑱ Pony Hollow Trail

Endpoints: Town of Elkader
Location: Clayton County
Length: 4 miles
Surface: Crushed stone

Contact:
Don R. Menken, Director
Clayton County Conservation Board
RR 2, Box 65A
Elkader, IA 52043
319-245-1516

⑲ Praeri Rail Trail

Endpoints: Roland to Zearing
Location: Story County
Length: 10.5 miles
Surface: Crushed stone

Contact:
Robert Pinneke, Director
Story County Conservation
Board
McFarland Park
R.R. 2, Box 272V
Ames, IA 50010
515-377-2229

⑳ Puddle Jumper Trail

Endpoints: Orange City to Alton
Location: Sioux County
Length: 2.5 miles
Surface: Crushed stone

Contact:
Don Schreur
City Administrator
Parks and Recreation Director
City Hall
Orange City, IA 51041
712-737-4885

㉑ Raccoon River Valley Trail

Endpoints: Waukee to Yale
Location: Dallas and Guthrie
Counties
Length: 33 miles
Surface: Asphalt

Dallas County Section

Contact:
Jeff Logsdon, Director
Dallas County Conservation
Department
1477 K Avenue
Perry, IA 50220
515-465-3577

Guthrie County Section

Contact:
Joe Hanner, Director
Guthrie County Conservation
Board
R.R.2, Box 4A17
Panora, IA 50216
515-755-3061

22 Ringgold Trailway

Endpoints: Mt. Ayr
Location: Ringgold County
Length: 2 miles
Surface: Original ballast

Contact:
Rick Hawkins, Director
Ringgold County Conservation
Board
Box 83A, RR 1
Mt. Ayr, IA 50854
515-464-2787

23 Russell White Nature Trail

Endpoints: South of Lanesboro
Location: Carroll County
Length: 3.8 miles
Surface: Original ballast and grass

Contact:
David J. Olson, Director
Carroll County Conservation
Board
RR 1, Box 240A
Carroll, IA 51401
712-792-4614

24 Sauk Trail

Endpoints: Carroll to Lake View
Location: Carroll and Sac
Counties
Length: 13 miles of 33.2-mile
trail is on abandoned rail line
Surface: Asphalt and crushed
limestone

Carroll County Section

Contact:
David J. Olson, Director
Carroll County Conservation
Board
R.R. 1, Box 240A
Carroll, IA 51401
712-792-4614

Sac County Section

Contact:
Chris Bass, Director
Sac County Conservation Board
2970 280th Street
Sac City, IA 50583
712-662-4530

25 Shell Rock River Trail

Endpoints: Clarksville to Shell Rock
Location: Butler County
Length: 5.2 miles
Surface: Crushed limestone

 on certain sections

Contact:
Steve Brunsma, Director
Butler County Conservation Board
R.R. 1
Clarksville, IA 50619
319-278-4237

26 Shimek Forest Trail

Endpoints: Shimek State Forest
Location: Lee County
Length: 3 miles
Surface: Grass and original ballast

Contact:
Jim Zohrer, Trails Coordinator
Iowa Department of Natural Resources
Wallace State Office Building
Des Moines, IA 50319
515-281-3449

27 Three Rivers Trail

Endpoints: Eagle Grove to Rolfe
Location: Wright, Humbolt and Pocohontas Counties
Length: 12 miles (will be 39 miles when completed)
Surface: Crushed limestone and original ballast

Contact:
Dan Gifford
Resource Coordinator
Humbolt County Conservation Board
Courthouse
Dakota City, IA 50529
515-332-4087

28 Wabash Trace Nature Trail

Endpoints: Council Bluffs to Blanchard
Location: Pottawattamie, Mills, Freemont and Page Counties
Length: 64 miles
Surface: Crushed limestone and original ballast

 on certain sections

Contact:
Bill Hillman
Vice President of Southwest Iowa Nature Trails Inc.
Box 581
Shenandoah, IA 51601
712-264-4444

㉙ Winneshiek County Trail

Endpoints: Calmar to Winneshiek County line
Location: Winneshiek County
Length: 16 miles
Surface: Crushed limestone

 on certain sections

Contact:
David Oestmann, Director
Winneshiek County
Conservation Board
R.R. 2, Box 102
Fort Atkinson, IA 52144
319-534-7145

㉚ Yellow River Forest Trail

Endpoints: Yellow River State Forest (6 miles north of Marquette)
Location: Allamakee County
Length: 4 miles
Surface: Grass and original ballast

Contact:
Jim Zohrer, Trails Coordinator
Iowa Department of Natural Resources
Wallace State Office Building
Des Moines, IA 50319
515-281-3449

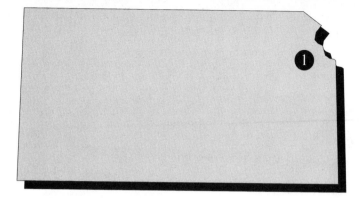

❶ *Lawrence Trail*

Endpoints: City of Lawrence
Location: Douglas County
Length: 1 mile
Surface: Limestone screenings

Contact:
Fred DeVictor, Director
Lawrence Parks and Recreation
Department
Box 708
Lawrence, KS 66044
913-832-3000 ext. 3450

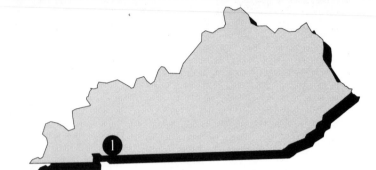

❶ *Cadiz Railroad Trail*

Endpoints: City of Cadiz
Location: Trigg County
Length: 1.5 miles
Surface: Asphalt

Contact:
Stan White
Cadiz Railroad Trail Committee
P.O. Drawer B
Cadiz, KY 42211
502-522-8483

MAINE

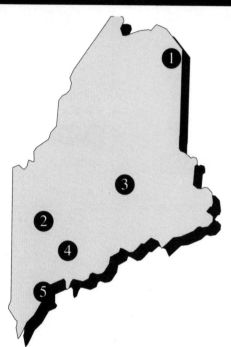

❶ *Aroostook Valley Right-of-Way*

Endpoints: Washburn to Caribou and Sweden
Location: Aroostook County
Length: 18 miles
Surface: Original ballast

Contact:
Scott D. Ramsey, Supervisor
Off Road Vehicles
Bureau of Parks
Dept. of Conservation, #22
Augusta, ME 04333
207-289-4957

❷ *Jay-to-Farmington Trail*

Endpoints: Jay to Farmington
Location: Franklin County
Length: 14 miles
Surface: Gravel

Contact:
Scott D. Ramsey, Supervisor
Off Road Vehicles
Bureau of Parks
Dept. of Conservation, #22
Augusta, ME 04333
207-289-4957

➌ Lagrange Right-of-way Trail

Endpoints: South Lagrange to Medford
Location: Piscataquis and Penobscot Counties
Length: 12 miles
Surface: Packed gravel

Contact:
Scott D. Ramsey, Supervisor
Off Road Vehicles
Bureau of Parks
Dept. of Conservation, #22
Augusta, ME 04333
207-289-4957

➍ Old Narrow Gauge Volunteer Nature Trail

Endpoints: Town of Randolph
Location: Kennebec County
Length: 2.4 miles
Surface: Original ballast

 on certain sections

Contact:
Town Clerk
Town Office
128 Water Street
Randolph, ME 04346
207-582-5808

➎ South Portland Greenbelt South

Endpoints: South Portland
Location: Cumberland County
Length: 2.5 miles
Surface: Asphalt

Contact:
Jerre Bryant, City Manager
City Hall
25 Cottage Road
South Portland, ME 04106
207-767-3201

MARYLAND

❶ Baltimore and Annapolis Trail

Endpoints: Glen Burnie to the Severn River
Location: Ann Arundel County
Length: 13.3 miles
Surface: Asphalt

Contact:
Dave Dionne, Superintendent
Baltimore and Annapolis Trail Park
P.O. Box 1007
Severna Park, MD 21146
301-222-6244

❷ Northern Central Railroad Trail

Endpoints: Ashland to Pennsylvania line near New Freedom, PA
Location: Baltimore County
Length: 20 miles
Surface: Crushed stone

 on certain sections

Contact:
Dave Davis, Manager
Gunpowder Falls State Park
P.O. Box 5032
Glen Arm, MD 21057
301-592-2897

❸ Number Nine Trolley Line

Endpoints: Baltimore
Location: Baltimore County
Length: 1.5 miles
Surface: Asphalt

Contact:
Charles Kines
Regional Superintendent
Baltimore County Department of Recreation and Parks
301 Washington Avenue
Towson, MD 21204
410-887-3829

MASSACHUSETTS

❶ *Cape Cod Rail Trail*

Endpoints: Dennis to Eastham
Location: Barnstable County
Length: 19.6 miles (2 miles
on-street in Orleans)
Surface: Asphalt with parallel
dirt treadway

Contact:
Steve Nicolle, Park Manager
Nickerson State Park
Main Street
Brewster, MA 02631
508-896-3491

❷ *Falmouth Shining Sea Trail*

Endpoints: Falmouth to Woods
Hole
Location: Barnstable County
Length: 3.2 miles
Surface: Asphalt with parallel
dirt treadway

Contact:
Kevin Lynch
P.O. Box 372
Peaticket, MA 02536
508-968-5859

❸ *Five Colleges Bikeway*

Endpoints: Amherst to
Northampton
Location: Hampshire County
Length: 9 miles
Surface: Concrete

Contact:
Daniel O'Brien
Bikeway and Rail Trail Planner
Department of Environmental
Management
Division of Resource
Conservation
100 Cambridge Street
Room 1404
Boston, MA 02202
617-727-3160 Ext. 557

❹ Minuteman Bikeway

Endpoints: Arlington, Lexington and Bedford
Location: Middlesex County
Length: 11 miles
Surface: Asphalt

Contact:
Alan McClennen, Jr.
Director of Planning and
Community Development
Town Hall
730 Massachusetts Avenue
Arlington, MA 02174
617-646-1000 Ext. 4130

❺ Northampton Bikeway

Endpoints: City of Northampton
Location: Hampshire County
Length: 2.6 miles
Surface: Asphalt

Contact:
George Andrikidis
Northampton Department of
Public Works
125 Locust Street
Northampton, MA 01060
413-586-6950

❻ Quarries Footpath

Endpoints: Quincy Quarries
Historic Site
Location: Norfolk County
Length: 1 mile
Surface: Dirt

Contact:
Peter Church or Steve Ovellette
Quincy Quarries Historic Site
Metropolitan District
Commission
695 Hillside Street
Milton, MA 02186
617-698-1802

❼ Southwest Corridor Park

Endpoints: City of Boston
Location: Suffolk County
Length: 5 miles
Surface: Asphalt

Contact:
Allan Morris, Parkland Manager
Southwest Corridor Park
38 New Heath Street
Jamaica Plain, MA 02130
617-727-0057

MICHIGAN

❶ Battle Creek Linear Park

Endpoints: City of Battle Creek
Location: Calhoun County
Length: .5-mile of 17-mile trail is on abandoned rail line
Surface: Asphalt

Contact:
Linn Kracht, Recreation
Superintendent
City of Battle Creek
Parks and Recreation
Department
124 East Michigan Avenue
Battle Creek, MI 49017
616-966-3431

❷ Baw Beese Trail

Endpoints: City of Hillsdale
Location: Hillsdale County
Length: 2 miles (will be 6 miles when completed)
Surface: Original ballast

Contact:
Mark Reynolds
Recreation Director
43 McCollum
Hillsdale, MI 49242
517-437-3579

54

❸ Bay Hampton Rail Trail

Endpoints: Bay City to Hampton Township
Location: Bay County
Length: 4 miles of 6-mile trail is on abandoned rail line
Surface: Asphalt

Contacts:
Al McFadyen
City of Bay City
301 Washington Street
Bay City, MI 48708
517-894-8154

Dick Hart
Hampton Township
P.O.Box 187
Bay City, MI 48707
517-893-7541

❹ Beaver Pete's Trail

Endpoints: Dickinson/ Menominee County line to Iron Mountain
Location: Dickinson County
Length: 14.5 miles of 20-mile trail is on abandoned rail line
Surface: Original ballast

Contact:
Allen Keto
Assistant Area Forest Ranger
Norway Forest Area
Copper Country State Forest
US-2
Norway, MI 49870
906-563-9247

❺ Bergland to Sidnaw Trail

Endpoints: Bergland to Sidnaw
Location: Ontonogan and Houghton Counties
Length: 45 miles
Surface: Original ballast

Contact:
Martin Nelson
Area Forest Manager
Copper Country State Forest
PO Box 400
Baraga, MI 49908
906-353-6651

❻ Bill Nicholls Trail

Endpoints: McKeever to Houghton
Location: Ontonagon and Houghton Counties
Length: 40.6 miles of 55-mile trail is on abandoned rail line
Surface: Original ballast

Contact:
Duane St. Ours
District Fire and Recreation Specialist
Copper Country State Forest
P.O.Box 440
Baraga, MI 49908
906-353-6651

❼ Chelsea Hospital Fitness Trail

Endpoints: Village of Chelsea
Location: Washtenaw County
Length: .25-mile of 1-mile trail is on abandoned rail line
Surface: Wood chips

Contact:
Phillip Boham, Vice President
Chelsea Community Hospital
775 S. Main
Chelsea, MI 48118
313-475-3998

❽ Coalwood Trail

Endpoints: Haywire Trail at Shingleton to Chatham
Location: Alger County
Length: 24 miles
Surface: Original ballast

Contacts:
Dick Andersen
Assistant Ranger
Munising Ranger District
Hiawatha National Forest
400 East Munising
Munising, MI 49862
906-387-2512

Bruce Veneberg
Area Forest Manager
Shingleton Forest Area
Lake Superior State Forest
M-28
Shingleton, MI 49884
906-452-6227

❾ Felch Grade Trail

Endpoints: Narenta to Felch
Location: Menominee, Delta and Dickinson Counties
Length: 27.5 miles of 45-mile trail is on abandoned rail line
Surface: Original ballast

Contact:
Allen Keto
Assistant Area Forest Ranger
Norway Forest Area
Copper Country State Forest
US-2
Norway, MI 49870
906-563-9247

❿ Frank N. Anderson Trail

Endpoints: Bay City State Park
Location: Bay County
Length: .75 mile
Surface: Asphalt

Contact:
Karen Gillispie
Bay City State Park
3582 State Park Drive
Bay City, MI 48706
517-684-3020

⑪ *Freda Trail*

Endpoints: Freda to Bill
Nicholls Trail
Location: Houghton County
Length: 11.2 miles
Surface: Original ballast

Contact:
Duane St. Ours
District Fire and Recreation
Specialist
Copper Country State Forest
P.O.Box 440
Baraga, MI 49908
906-353-6651

⑫ *Grand Marais Trail*

Endpoints: Shingleton to Grand
Marais
Location: Alger and Schoolcraft
Counties
Length: 13 miles of 41.7-mile
trail is on abandoned rail line
Surface: Original ballast

![snowmobile icon]

Contact:
Bruce Veneberg
Area Forest Manager
Shingleton Forest Area
Lake Superior State Forest
M-28
Shingleton, MI 49884
906-452-6227

⑬ *Hancock/Calumet Trail*

Endpoints: Hancock to Calumet
Location: Houghton County
Length: 12.5 miles
Surface: Original ballast

Contact:
Duane St. Ours
District Fire and Recreation
Specialist
Copper Country State Forest
P.O.Box 440
Baraga, MI 49908
906-353-6651

⑭ *Hart-Montague Bicycle Trail State Park*

Endpoints: Hart to Montague
Location: Oceana and
Muskegon Counties
Length: 22.5 miles
Surface: Asphalt

![horse icon] on certain sections

Contact:
Peter Lundborg
Silver Lake State Park
Route 1, Box 254
Mears, MI 49436
616-873-3083

15 Haywire Trail

Endpoints: Manistique to Shingleton
Location: Schoolcraft and Alger Counties
Length: 36 miles
Surface: Original ballast

Contacts:
Dick Andersen
Assistant Ranger
Munising Ranger District
Hiawatha National Forest
400 East Munising
Munising, MI 49862
906-387-2512

Bruce Veneberg
Area Forest Manager
Shingleton Forest Area
Lake Superior State Forest
M-28
Shingleton, MI 49884
906-452-6227

16 Huron Forest Snowmobile Trails

Endpoints: Huron National Forest
Location: Alcona and Oscoda Counties
Length: 11 miles of 95-mile trail system is on abandoned rail line
Surface: Dirt

 on certain sections

Contact:
Joe Gates, Assistant Ranger
Harrisville Ranger District
Huron National Forest
PO Box 286
Harrisville, MI 48740
517-724-6471

17 Iron's Area Tourist Association Snowmobile Trail

Endpoints: Manistee National Forest
Location: Lake and Manistee Counties
Length: 22 miles
Surface: Original ballast

Contact:
Greg Peterson, Forester
USDA Forest Service
1658 Manistee Highway
Manistee, MI 49660
616-723-2211

⑱ *Iron Range Trails*

Endpoints: Crystal Falls to Iron River Trail
Location: Iron County
Length: 25 miles
Surface: Original ballast

Endpoints: Crystal Falls to Stager Trail
Location: Iron County
Length: 11 miles
Surface: Original ballast

Endpoints: Beechwood to Sidnaw Trail
Location: Iron County
Length: 7 miles of 48-mile trail is on abandoned rail line
Surface: Original ballast

Contact:
Duane St. Ours
District Fire and Recreation Specialist
Copper Country State Forest
P.O.Box 440
Baraga, MI 49908
906-353-6651

⑲ *Jordan Valley Snowmobile Trail*

Endpoints: Jordan Valley Area
Location: Charlevoix and Antrim Counties
Length: 8 miles of 33-mile trail is on abandoned rail line
Surface: Original ballast

Contact:
Duane Hoffman
District Fire and Recreation Specialist
Mackinaw State Forest
P.O.Box 660
Gaylord, MI 49735
517-732-3541

⑳ *Kal-Haven Trail Sesquicentennial State Park*

Endpoints: Kalamazoo to South Haven
Location: Kalamazoo and Van Buren Counties
Length: 34.1 miles
Surface: Crushed stone

on certain sections

Contact:
David Marsh
Van Buren State Park
23960 Ruggles Road
South Haven, MI 49090
616-637-4984

21 Kent Trails

Endpoints: Grand Rapids Area
Location: Kent County
Length: 6.5 miles of 15-mile trail is on abandoned rail line
Surface: Asphalt

Contact:
Roger Sabine
Kent County Road and Park Commission
1500 Scribner, N.W.
Grand Rapids, MI 49504
616-242-6948

22 Keweenaw Trail

Endpoints: Houghton to Calumet
Location: Houghton County
Length: 21 miles
Surface: Original ballast

Contact:
Duane St. Ours
District Fire and Recreation Specialist
Copper Country State Forest
P.O.Box 440
Baraga, MI 49908
906-353-6651

23 Kiwanis Trail

Endpoints: Adrian to Tecumseh
Location: Lenawee County
Length: 8.5 miles
Surface: Asphalt and original ballast

 on certain sections

Contact:
Ray Maxe
Adrian City Hall
100 E. Church Street
Adrian, MI 49221
517-263-2161

24 Lakelands Trail State Park

Endpoints: Western Section: Jackson to Hamburg
Eastern Section: South Lyon to Wixom
Location: Jackson, Ingham, Livingston and Oakland Counties
Length: 29 miles (west), 7 miles (east), (will be 36 miles when completed; scheduled to open in 1993)
Surface: Original ballast now, crushed slag when completed

Contact:
Jon LaBossiere
Pinckney Recreation Area
8555 Silver Hill, Route 1
Pinckney, MI 48169
313-426-4913

25 Lakeside Trail

Endpoints: Village of Spring Lake
Location: Ottawa County
Length: 1.75 miles
Surface: Asphalt

Contact:
Eric DeLong, Village Manager
Village of Spring Lake
102 W. Savidge Street
Spring Lake, MI 49456
616-842-1393

26 Lansing River Trail

Endpoints: City of Lansing
Location: Ingham County
Length: .5-mile of 6-mile trail is on abandoned rail line
Surface: Asphalt

Contact:
Peter Stoughton
Parks and Recreation
124 W. Michigan
Lansing, MI 48933
517-483-4277

27 Little Lake-Chatham Snowmobile Trail

Endpoints: Chatham to Little Lake
Location: Alger and Marquette Counties
Length: 15.9 miles of 26-mile trail is on abandoned rail line
Surface: Original ballast

Contact:
Bill Brondyke
Area Forest Manager
Gwinn Forest Area
410 W. M-35
Gwinn, MI 49841
906-346-9201

28 Mackinaw/Alanson Trail

Endpoints: Mackinaw to Alanson
Location: Emmett and Cheboygan Counties
Length: 24 miles
Surface: Original ballast

Contact:
Duane Hoffman
District Fire and Recreation Specialist
Mackinaw State Forest
P.O.Box 660
Gaylord, MI 49735
517-732-3541

㉙ McClure Riverfront Park

Endpoints: City of Albion
Location: Calhoun County
Length: .2-mile
Surface: Wood chips

Contact:
Susan Rieske
Superintendent of Parks
City Hall
112 W. Cass
Albion, MI 49224
517-629-5535

㉚ Nordhouse Dunes Trail System

Endpoints: Manistee National
Forest, Nordhouse Dunes
Wilderness
Location: Mason County
Length: 4 miles of 15-mile trail
is on abandoned rail line
Surface: Sand

Contact:
Greg Peterson, Forester
USDA Forest Service
1658 Manistee Highway
Manistee, MI 49660
616-723-2211

㉛ Paint Creek Trail

Endpoints: Lake Orion to
Rochester
Location: Oakland County
Length: 10.5 miles
Surface: Crushed stone

on certain sections

Contact:
Linda Gorecki
Trailways Coordinator
Paint Creek Trailways
Commission
4393 Collins Road
Rochester, MI 48064
313-651-9260

㉜ Pere Marquette Rail-Trail of Mid-Michigan

Endpoints: Midland to Clare
Location: Midland and Isabella
Counties
Length: 30 miles
Surface: Asphalt and crushed
stone

on certain sections

Contact:
Bill Gibson, Director
Midland County Parks and
Recreation Department
220 W. Ellsworth Street
Midland, MI 48640-5194
517-832-6870

㉝ Peshekee to Clowry ORV Trail

Endpoints: Near Champion
Location: Marquette County
Length: 6.1 miles
Surface: Original ballast

Contact:
Dennis Nezich
Area Forest Manager
Ishpeming Forest Area
Escanaba River State Forest
1985 US-41
Ishpeming, MI 49849
906-485-1031

㉞ Republic/Champion Grade Trail

Endpoints: Champion to Republic
Location: Marquette County
Length: 8 miles
Surface: Original ballast

Contact:
Dennis Nezich
Area Forest Manager
Ishpeming Forest Area
Escanaba River State Forest
1985 US-41
Ishpeming, MI 49849
906-485-1031

㉟ Rivertrail Park

Endpoints: City of Portland
Location: Ionia County
Length: 1.7 miles of 2.25-mile trail is on abandoned rail line
Surface: Asphalt
Scheduled to open in 1993

Contact:
Mary Scheurer
City of Portland
Parks and Recreation Department
259 Kent Street
Portland, MI 48875
517-647-7985

㊱ Skegemog Lake Pathway

Endpoints: Skegemog Lake Wildlife Area
Location: Kalkaska and Antrim Counties
Length: .5-mile of .75-mile trail is on abandoned rail line
Surface: Original ballast

Contact:
Dennis Vitton
Area Forest Manager
2089 Birch
Kalkaska, MI 49646
616-258-9471

③⑦ Soo/Strongs Trail

Endpoints: Sault Ste. Marie west to Raco
Location: Chippewa County
Length: 16.7 miles of 20-mile trail is on abandoned rail line
Surface: Original ballast

Contact:
Mike Renner
Sault Ste. Marie Forest Area
Lake Superior State Forest
P.O. Box 798
Sault Ste. Marie, MI 49783
906-293-5131

Endpoints: Raco west to Strongs
Location: Chippewa County
Length: 12.3 miles
Surface: Original ballast

Contact:
Roger Jewell, District Ranger
Sault Ste. Marie Ranger District
Hiawatha National Forest
4000 I-75, Business Spur
Sault Ste. Marie, MI 49783
906-635-5311

③⑧ Spring Brook Pathway

Endpoints: Jordan River State Forest and Mackinaw State Forest
Location: Charlevoix County
Length: .75-mile of 6.25-mile trail is on abandoned rail line
Surface: Original ballast

Contact:
Jerry Lawrence
Area Forest Manager
Gaylord Field Office
P.O. Box 667
Gaylord, MI 49735
517-732-3541

㊴ State Line Trail

Endpoints: Marenisco east to Stager
Location: Iron and Gogebic Counties
Length: 87.1 miles
Surface: Original ballast

 on certain sections

Endpoints: Marenisco west to Wakefield
Location: Gogebic County
Length: 15 miles of 20-mile trail is on abandoned rail line
Surface: Original ballast

Contact:
Duane St. Ours
District Fire and Recreation Specialist
Copper Country State Forest
P.O.Box 440
Baraga, MI 49908
906-353-6651

Joey M. Spano
West Bloomfield Parks and Recreation Commission
3325 Middlebelt Road
West Bloomfield, MI 48323
313-334-5660

㊵ Traverse Area Recreation Trail (TART)

Endpoints: Traverse City to Acme
Location: Grand Traverse County
Length: 2.75 miles (will be 7.75 miles when completed in 1993)
Surface: Asphalt

Contact:
Mike Dillenbeck, Manager
Grand Traverse County Road Commission
3949 Silver Lake Road
Traverse City, MI 49684
616-922-4848

㊶ Watersmeet/ Land O'Lakes Trail

Endpoints: Watersmeet to Wisconsin state line near Land O'Lakes
Location: Gogebic County
Length: 8 miles
Surface: Original ballast

Contact:
Wayne Petterson
District Ranger
U.S. Forest Service
P.O. Box 276
Watersmeet, MI 49969
906-358-4551

42 *Wellston Area Tourist Association Snowmobile Trail*

Endpoints: Manistee National Forest
Location: Manistee County
Length: 6 miles of 50-miles trail system is on abandoned rail line
Surface: Original ballast

Contact:
Greg Peterson, Forester
Manistee Ranger District
1658 Manistee Highway
Manistee, MI 49660
616-723-2211

43 *West Bloomfield Trail Network*

Endpoints: Township of West Bloomfield
Location: Oakland County
Length: 4.3 miles of 5.3 miles on abandoned rail line
Surface: Crushed stone

Contact:
Joey M. Spano
West Bloomfield Parks and Recreation Commission
3325 Middlebelt Road
West Bloomfield, MI 48323
313-334-5660

44 *West Campus Bicycle Path*

Endpoints: Eastern Michigan University
Location: Washtenaw County
Length: 1 mile
Surface: Asphalt

Contact:
Dan Klenczar
Physical Plant
Eastern Michigan University
Ypsilanti, MI 48197
313-487-4194

66

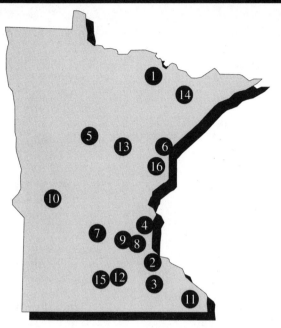

❶ *Arrowhead State Trail*

Endpoints: Kabetogama State Forest
Location: St. Louis County
Length: 9.5 miles of 131-mile trail is on abandoned rail line
Surface: Original ballast

Black Duck Trail Segment

Length: 5 miles

Myrtle Lake Trail Segment

Length: 4.5 miles

Contact:
Ron Potter, Area Supervisor
Minnesota Department
of Natural Resources
Trails and Waterways
P.O. Box 388
218-753-6256

❷ Cannon Valley Trail

Endpoints: Cannon Falls to Red Wing
Location: Goodhue County
Length: 19.7 miles
Surface: Asphalt

Contact:
Bruce Blair, Superintendent
Cannon Valley Trail
City Hall
306 West Mill Street
Cannon Falls, MN 55009
507-263-3954

❸ Douglas State Trail

Endpoints: Northwest of Rochester to Pine Island
Location: Olmstead and Goodhue Counties
Length: 12.5 miles
Surface: Asphalt

Contact:
Joel Wagar
Trails and Waterways Area Manager
Minnesota Department of Natural Resources
P.O. Box 6247
Rochester, MN 55903
507-285-7176

❹ Gateway Segment of the Willard Munger Trail

Endpoints: Pine Point Regional Park to St. Paul
Location: Washington and Ramsey Counties
Surface: Asphalt
Length: 16.9 mile trail with 9.5-mile parallel dirt treadway for horses and carriages

Contact:
Larry Killien
Area Supervisor
Minnesota Department of Natural Resources
Trails and Waterways
1200 Warner Road
St. Paul, MN 55106
612-772-7935

❺ Heartland State Trail

Endpoints: Park Rapids to Cass Lake
Location: Hubbard and Cass Counties
Length: 50 miles
Surface: Asphalt with parallel dirt treadway (Park Rapids to Walker) and original ballast

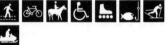

Contact:
Pat Tangeman
Heartland State Trail
P.O. Box 112
Nevis, MN 56467
218-652-4054

6 Lakewalk

Endpoints: City of Duluth
Location: St. Louis County
Length: 1.5 miles (will be 3 miles when completed)
Surface: Asphalt with parallel wooden boardwalk

Contacts:
Sue Moyer, Director
Duluth Parks and Recreation Department
Room 330
City Hall
411 W. First Street
Duluth, MN 55802
218-723-3337

Duluth Convention and Visitor's Bureau
100 Lake Place Drive
Duluth, MN 55802
218-722-4011

7 Luce Line Trail

Endpoints: Plymouth to Cosmos
Location: Hennepin, Carver, McLeod and Meeker Counties
Length: 30 miles developed from Plymouth to Winsted (will be 65 miles when completed)
Surface: Crushed limestone with parallel dirt treadway

 on certain sections

Contact:
Richard Schmidt
Trails and Waterways Technician
3980 Watertown Road
Maple Plain, MN 55359
612-475-0371

8 Minnehaha Trail

Endpoints: Historic Fort Snelling State Park to south of Minnehaha Park
Location: Hennepin County
Length: 2 miles of 5-mile trail is on abandoned rail ine
Surface: Asphalt

Contact:
John Lilly
Assistant Park Manager
Fort Snelling State Park
Highway 5 and Post Road
St. Paul, MN 55111
612-725-2390

⑨ Minnetonka Loop

Endpoints: City of Minnetonka
Location: Hennepin County
Length: 5.1 miles of 10-mile trail is on abandoned rail line (will be 30 miles when completed)
Surface: Crushed stone

Contact:
Bob Hill, Loop Trail Coordinator
City of Minnetonka
14600 Minnetonka Boulevard
Minnetonka, MN 55345
612-938-7245

⑩ Minnewaska Snowmobile Trail

Endpoints: Starbuck to Villard
Location: Pope County
Length: 8.9 miles of 25-mile trail is on abandoned rail line
Surface: Original ballast

![snowmobile icon]

Contact:
Bill Anderson, Trail Manager
Douglas Area Trails Association
P.O. Box 112
Alexandria, MN 56308
612-834-2033

⑪ Root River State Trail

Endpoints: Fountain to Money Creek Woods
Location: Fillmore and Houston Counties
Length: 37.4 miles
Surface: Asphalt and grass

 on certain sections only

Contact:
Craig Blommer
Trails and Waterways Area Manager
Minnesota Department of Natural Resources
P.O. Box 6247
Rochester, MN 55903
507-285-7176

⑫ Sakatah Singing Hills State Trail

Endpoints: Faribault to Mankato
Location: Rice, LeSueur and Blue Earth Counties
Length: 38.6 miles
Surface: Crushed stone

![activity icons]

Contact:
Randy Schoeneck
Trail Technician
Elysian Wayside, P.O. Box 11
Elysian, MN 56028
507-267-4772

⑬ *Soo Line Trail*

Endpoints: Cass Lake to Moose Lake State Park
Location: Cass, Aitkin and Carlton Counties
Length: 120 miles
Surface: Original ballast

Chippewa National Forest Section

Contact:
Bill Stocker, District Ranger
Chippewa National Forest
Rt. 3 Box 219
Cass Lake, MN 56633
218-335-2283

Cass County Section

Contact:
Dan Marcum, Field Supervisor
Cass County Lands Department
P.O. Box 25
Pine Mountain Professional Building
Backus, MN 56435
218-947-3338

Aitkin County Section

in summer only

Contact:
Roger Howard
County Land Commission
Courthouse
Aitkin, MN 56431
218-927-2102

Carlton County Section

Contact:
Milo Rasfensen, Land Commissioner
Carlton County Lands Department
Box 130
Carlton, MN 55718
218-384-4281

⓮ *Taconite State Trail*

Endpoints: Bear Island State Forest
Location: St. Louis County
Length: 16 miles of 168-mile trail is on abandoned rail line

Star Lake to Murray Spur

Length: 3 miles
Surface: Original ballast and gravel

Putnam Lake Trail Segment

Length: 9 miles
Surface: Original ballast

Fishing Lakes Trail Segment

Length: 4 miles
Surface: Original ballast

Contact:
Ron Potter, Area Supervisor
Minnesota Department of Natural Resources
Trails and Waterways
P.O. Box 388
Tower, MN 55790
218-753-6256

⓯ *West Mankato Trail*

Endpoints: Mankato City
Location: Blue Earth County
Length: 1.5 miles
Surface: Asphalt

Contact:
Floyd Roberts
Parks Superintendent
City of Mankato Parks and Forestry
P.O. Box 3328
Mankato, MN 56002-3328
507-387-8650

⓰ *Willard Munger State Trail*

Endpoints: Hinckley to Barnum, Carlton to West Duluth and Wrenshall to Wisconsin state line
Location: Pine, Carlton and St. Louis Counties
Length: 55.5 miles
Surface: Asphalt and original ballast

 on certain sections

Contact:
Kevin Arends
Minnesota Department of Natural Resources
Trails and Waterways
Route 2, 701 South Kenwood
Moose Lake, MN 55767
218-485-8647

MISSISSIPPI

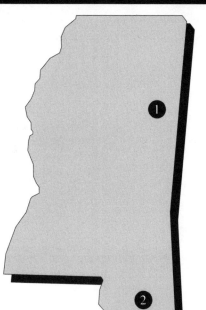

❶ Catherine "Kitty" Bryan Dill Memorial Bikeway

Endpoints: West Point
Location: Clay County
Length: 1.2 miles
Surface: Concrete

Contact:
Dewel G. Brasher, Jr.
City Manager
P.O. Box 1117
West Point, MS 39773
601-494-2573

❷ Tuxachanie National Recreation Trail

Endpoints: DeSoto National Forest
Location: Harrison County
Length: 5 miles of 17-mile trail is on abandoned rail line
Surface: Original ballast

Contact:
Roy Smith, District Ranger
Biloxi Ranger District
U.S. Forest Service
251 Highway 49 South
P.O. Box 62
McHenry, MS 39561
601-928-5291

MISSOURI

❶ *Frisco Greenway*

Endpoints: Joplin to Webb City
Location: Joplin County
Length: 4 miles
Surface: Crushed limestone and original ballast

 on certain sections

Contact:
Cliff Walker, President
Joplin Trails Coalition
2601 North Rangeline
Joplin, MO 64801
417-781-1664

❷ *Katy Trail State Park*

Endpoints: Machens to Sedalia
Location: St. Charles, Warren, Montgomery, Callaway, Boone, Howard, Cooper and Pettis Counties
Length: 122 miles developed from Machens to Treloar and Jefferson City to Sedalia (will be 200 miles when completed)
Surface: Crushed stone

Contact:
John Balkenbush
Superintendent
Katy Trail State Park
Missouri Department of Natural Resources
Box 176
Jefferson City, MO 65102
314-751-2479

③ M.K.T. Nature/Fitness Trail

Endpoints: City of Columbia
Location: Boone County
Length: 4.7 miles
Surface: Crushed limestone

Contact:
City of Columbia
Parks and Recreation
P.O. Box N
Columbia, MO 65205
314-874-7201

④ West Alton Trail

Endpoints: West Alton to Riverlands
Location: St. Charles County
Length: 1 mile
Surface: Original ballast

Contact:
Bill Kranz
Gateway Trailnet, Inc.
7185 Manchester Road
St. Louis, MO 63143
314-644-0315

MONTANA

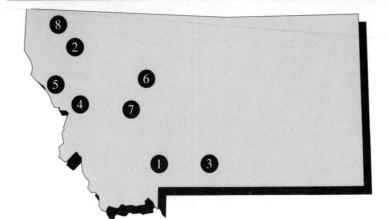

❶ *Gallagator Linear Trail*

Endpoints: Town of Bozeman
Location: Gallatin County
Length: 1.5 miles
Surface: Gravel and original ballast

Contact:
Sue Harkin
Bozeman Recreation
Department
P.O. Box 640
Bozeman, MT 59715
406-587-4724

❷ *Great Northern Rail Trail*

Endpoints: Kalispell to Marion
Location: Flathead County
Length: 1.25 miles developed in Kalispell (will be 23 miles when completed)
Surface: Gravel

Contact:
Mark Koeneker
President of Rails-to-Trails of
Northwest Montana
P.O. Box 1103
Kalispell, MT 59903
406-758-5241

❸ Heights Bike Trail

Endpoints: Billings
Location: Yellowstone County
Length: 3.5 miles
Surface: Gravel and dirt

Contact:
Mike Hink, Director
Department of Parks,
Recreation and Public Lands
510 N. Broadway
4th Floor Library
Billings, MT 59101
406-657-8366

❹ Kim Williams Nature Area

Endpoints: East of Missoula to
Hellgate Canyon
Location: Missoula County
Length: 2.5 miles
Surface: Original ballast

Contact:
Jim Van Fossen, Director
Missoula Parks and Recreation
Department
100 Hickory Street
Missoula, MT 59801
406-721-7275

❺ NorPac Trail

Endpoints: Lolo National Forest,
Saltese to the Idaho state line
Location: Mineral County
Length: 12.1 miles
Surface: Original ballast

Contact:
U.S. Forest Service
Superior Ranger District
Box 460
Superior, MT 59872
406-822-4233

❻ River's Edge Trail

Endpoints: Great Falls
Location: Cascade County
Length: 5.5 miles
Surface: Asphalt

on certain sections

Contact:
Doug Wicks
Friends of River's Edge Trail
P.O. Box 553
Great Falls, MT 59403
406-761-4966

❼ Spring Meadows Lake and Centennial Park Trail

Endpoints: Helena
Location: Lewis and Clark County
Length: 2.5 miles
Surface: Crushed stone

Contact:
Willa Hall, President
Gold County Rails-to-Trails
Box 434
Helena, MT 59624
406-443-0638

❽ Tobacco River Memorial Trail

Endpoints: Kootenai National Forest, Eureka City Park to Rexford
Location: Lincoln County
Length: 2 miles of 6-mile trail is on abandoned rail line
Surface: Gravel

Contact:
Eric Heyn
Resource Forester
Kootenai National Forest
1299 Highway 93 North
Eureka, MT 59917
406-296-2536

NEBRASKA

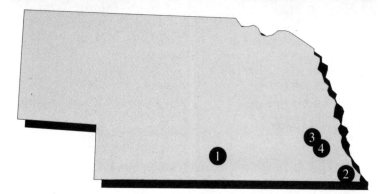

❶ Fort Kearny Hike-Bike Trail

Endpoints: Bassway Strip Wildlife Area to Fort Kearny State Recreation Area
Location: Kearney County
Length: 1.8 miles
Surface: Original ballast

Contact:
Eugene Hunt, Superintendent
Fort Kearney State Recreation Area
Route #4
Kearney, NE 68847
308-234-9513

❷ Iron Horse Trail Lake Park

Endpoints: Nemaha Natural Resources District Recreation Area
Location: Pawnee County
Length: 2.9 miles
Surface: Original ballast

Contact:
Paul Rohrbaugh
Nemaha Natural Resources District
125 Jackson
Tecumseh, NE 68450
402-335-3325

❸ MoPac Trail

Endpoints: City of Lincoln
Location: Lancaster County
Length: 4.2 miles (will be 29.2 miles when completed)
Surface: Concrete

Contact:
Robert Wright
Assistant Superintendent
City Parks and Recreation
2740 A Street
Lincoln, NE 68502
402-471-7847

❹ Rock Island Trail

Endpoints: City of Lincoln
Location: Lancaster County
Length: 2.4 miles developed (will be 7 miles when completed)
Surface: Concrete

 on undeveloped section

Contact:
Robert Wright
Assistant Superintendent
City Parks and Recreation
2740 A Street
Lincoln, NE 68502
402-471-7847

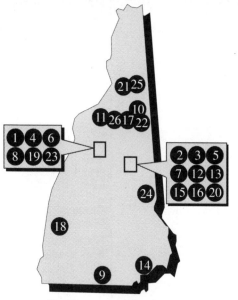

❶ Cedar Brook Trail

Endpoints: Trail #381, 2.4 miles from Kancamagus Highway on trail #277 to junction of Wilderness Trail and East Branch Pemigewasset River
Location: Pemigewasset Ranger District, White Mountain National Forest
Length: 1.5 miles of 5.7-mile trail is on abandoned rail line
Surface: Original ballast

Contact:
Jim Dimaio
District Ranger
RFD 3, Box 15
Plymouth, NH 03264
603-536-1310

❷ Dry River Trail

Endpoints: White Mountain National Forest
Location: Saco Ranger District
Length: 5.2 miles of 10.5-mile trail is on abandoned rail line
Surface: Original ballast

 on certain sections

Contact:
Robert M. Walker
District Ranger
Kancamagus Highway
RFD 1, Box 94
Conway, NH 03818
603-447-5448

❸ East Branch Trail

Endpoints: White Mountain National Forest
Location: Saco Ranger District
Length: 3 miles of 8-mile trail is on abandoned rail line
Surface: Original ballast

Contact:
Robert M. Walker
District Ranger
Kancamagus Highway
RFD 1, Box 94
Conway, NH 03818
603-447-5448

❹ Ethan Pond Trail

Endpoints: White Mountain National Forest, Trail #387, Crawford Notch State Park to Appalachian Mountain Club's Zealand Hut
Location: Pemigewasset Ranger District
Length: 1.5 miles of 5.6-mile trail is on abandoned rail line
Surface: Original ballast

Contact:
Jim Dimaio
District Ranger
RFD 3, Box 15
Plymouth, NH 03264
603-536-1310

❺ Flat Mountain Pond Trail

Endpoints: White Mountain National Forest
Location: Saco Ranger District
Length: 4 miles of 9-mile trail is on abandoned rail line
Surface: Original ballast

 on certain sections

Contact:
Robert M. Walker
District Ranger
Kancamagus Highway
RFD 1, Box 94
Conway, NH 03818
603-447-5448

❻ Franconia Brook Trail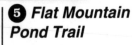

Endpoints: White Mountain National Forest, Trail #379, Franconia Falls area to 3/4 mile east of Mt. Garfield
Location: Pemigewasset Ranger District
Length: 5 miles of 7.2-mile trail is on abandoned rail line
Surface: Original ballast

Contact:
Jim Dimaio
District Ranger
RFD 3, Box 15
Plymouth, NH 03264
603-536-1310

❼ Guinea Pond Trail

Endpoints: White Mountain National Forest
Location: Saco Ranger District
Length: 4 miles
Surface: Original ballast

Contact:
Robert M. Walker
District Ranger
Kancamagus Highway
RFD 1, Box 94
Conway, NH 03818
603-447-5448

❽ Lincoln Woods Trail

Endpoints: Trail #383, Trailhead 1/4 mile east of Hancock Campground to Franconia Falls
Location: Pemigewasset Ranger District, White Mountain National Forest
Length: 2.7 miles
Surface: Original ballast

 on certain sections

Contact:
Jim Dimaio
District Ranger
RFD 3, Box 15
Plymouth, NH 03264
603-536-1310

❾ Mason Railroad Trail

Endpoints: Wilton to Massachusetts State Line at Townsend
Location: Hillsborough County
Length: 6.7 miles
Surface: Original ballast

Contact:
Liz Fletcher
Mason Conservation Commission
Mann House
Darling Hill Road
Mason, NH 03048
603-878-2070

❿ Moriah Brook Trail

Endpoints: White Mountain National Forest, 1/4 mile north of Wild River Campground to Carter Moriah Trail
Location: Evans Notch Ranger District
Length: 2 miles of 5.3-mile trail is on abandoned rail line
Surface: Original ballast

Contact:
Rollie Ortegon
District Ranger
RR 2, Box 2270
Bethel, ME 04217
207-824-2134

⑪ North Twin Trail

Endpoints: White Mountain National Forest, Top of North Twin Mountain to Forest Road 304 (Haystack Road)
Location: Ammonoosuc Ranger District
Length: 2 miles of 4.3 mile trail is on abandoned rail line
Surface: Dirt

Contact:
Paul A. Shaw, Jr.
District Ranger
P.O. Box 239
Bethlehem, NH 03574
603-869-2626

⑫ Oliverian Trail

Endpoints: White Mountain National Forest
Location: Saco Ranger District
Length: .5 mile of 3.5-mile trail is on abandoned rail line
Surface: Dirt

Contact:
Chester Russell, Forest Technician
Kancamagus Highway
RFD 1, Box 94
Conway, NH 03818
603-447-5448

⑬ Rob Brook Trail

Endpoints: White Mountain National Forest
Location: Saco Ranger District
Length: 1.8 miles of 2-mile trail is on abandoned rail line
Surface: Original ballast

Contact:
Robert M. Walker
District Ranger
Kancamagus Highway
RFD 1, Box 94
Conway, NH 03818
603-447-5448

⑭ Rockingham Recreational Trail

Endpoints: Fremont to Salem
Location: Rockingham County
Length: 22.5 miles
Surface: Original ballast

Contact:
Paul Gray, Chief
Department of Trails
New Hampshire Department of Resources and Economic Development
P.O. Box 856
Concord, NH 03302
603-271-3254

⑮ Rocky Branch Trail

Endpoints: White Mountain National Forest
Location: Saco Ranger District
Length: 6 miles of 9-mile trail is on abandoned rail line
Surface: Original ballast

Contact:
Robert M. Walker
District Ranger
Kancamagus Highway
RFD 1, Box 94
Conway, NH 03818
603-447-5448

⑯ Sawyer River Trail

Endpoints: White Mountain National Forest
Location: Saco Ranger District
Length: 4 miles
Surface: Original ballast

Contact:
Robert M. Walker
District Ranger
Kancamagus Highway
RFD 1, Box 94
Conway, NH 03818
603-447-5448

⑰ Shelburne Trail

Endpoints: White Mountain National Forest, Forest Road 12 (Wild River Road) to Route 2
Location: Evans Notch Ranger District
Length: 1 mile of 5-mile trail is on abandoned rail line
Surface: Original ballast

Contact:
Rollie Ortegon
District Ranger
RR 2, Box 2270
Bethel, ME 04217
207-824-2134

⑱ Sugar River Recreation Trail

Endpoints: Newport to Claremont
Location: Sullivan County
Length: 8 miles
Surface: Original ballast

Contact:
Paul Gray, Chief
Department of Trails
New Hampshire Department of Resources and Economic Development
P.O. Box 856
Concord, NH 03302
603-271-3254

⑲ Thoreau Falls Trail

Endpoints: White Mountain National Forest, Trail #385, Thoreau Falls to 1/2 mile south of North Fork
Location: Pemigewasset Ranger District
Length: 3.8 miles of 5.1-mile trail is on abandoned rail line
Surface: Original ballast

Contact:
Jim Dimaio
District Ranger
RFD 3, Box 15
Plymouth, NH 03264
603-536-1310

⑳ Upper Nanamocomuck Trail

Endpoints: White Mountain National Forest
Location: Saco Ranger District
Length: 2 miles of 9.3-mile trail is on abandoned rail line
Surface: Original ballast

Contact:
Robert M. Walker
District Ranger
Kancamagus Highway
RFD 1, Box 94
Conway, NH 03818
603-447-5448

㉑ West Milan Trail

Endpoints: White Mountain National Forest, Forest Road 104 to Forest Road 15 (Bog Dam Loop Road)
Location: Androscoggin Ranger District
Length: 4 miles of 12-mile trail is on abandoned rail line
Surface: Original ballast

Contact:
Katherine Bulchis
District Ranger
80 Glen Road
Gorham, NH 03581-1399
603-466-2713

㉒ Wild River Trail

Endpoints: White Mountain National Forest, Wild River Campground to Wildcat River Trail
Location: Evans Notch Ranger District
Length: 4 miles of 7.7-mile trail is on abandoned rail line
Surface: Original ballast

Contact:
Rollie Ortegon
District Ranger
RR 2, Box 2270
Bethel, ME 04217
207-824-2134

㉓ Wilderness Trail

Endpoints: White Mountain National Forest, Trail #383, Footbridge over Franconia Brook to 2/10 mile east of Shoalpond Brook
Location: Pemigewasset Ranger District
Length: 6 miles
Surface: Original ballast

Contact:
Jim Dimaio
District Ranger
RFD 3, Box 15
Plymouth, NH 03264
603-536-1310

㉔ Wolfeboro/ Sanbornville Recreational Trail

Endpoints: Wolfeboro to Sanbornville
Location: Carroll County
Length: 12 miles in two sections

Wolfeboro Section

Length: 1 mile
Surface: Crushed stone

Contact:
Town of Wolfeboro
P.O. Box 629
Wolfeboro, NH 03894
603-569-3900

Lake Wentworth State Park Section

Length: 11 miles
Surface: Dirt path alongside inactive tracks

 on certain sections
Speeders and handcars permitted on rails

Contact:
Paul Gray
Chief of Off-Highway Vehicles
New Hampshire Department of Resources and Economic Development
Trails Bureau
P.O. Box 856
Concord, NH 03302
603-271-3254

25 York Pond Trail

Endpoints: White Mountain National Forest, York Pond Fish Hatchery to Cabot Trail
Location: Androscoggin Ranger District
Length: 2.5 miles of 6.5-mile trail is on abandoned rail line
Surface: Original ballast

Contact:
Katherine Bulchis
District Ranger
80 Glen Road
Gorham, NH 03581-1399
603-466-2713

26 Zealand Trail

Endpoints: White Mountain National Forest, Twin Mountain, Zealand-Sugerloaf Campground, Forest Road 302
Location: Ammonoosuc Ranger District
Length: 2.5 miles
Surface: Gravel

Contact:
Roger Collins
Forest Technician
P.O. Box 239
Bethlehem, NH 03574
603-869-2626

NEW JERSEY

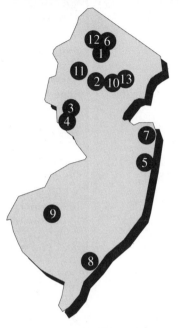

❶ Berkshire Valley Management Area Trail

Endpoints: Lake Hopatcong
Location: Morris County
Length: 3 miles
Surface: Cinder

 with permit only

Contact:
Jim Munson, Crew Supervisor
Black River Wildlife
Management Area
Box 52, North Road
Chester, NJ 07930
908-879-6252

❷ Black River Wildlife Management Area Trail

Endpoints: Chester Township
Location: Morris County
Length: 5 miles
Surface: Cinder

with permit only

Contact:
Jim Munson, Crew Supervisor
Black River WIldlife
Management Area
Box 52, North Road
Chester, NJ 07930
908-879-6252

❸ Capoolong Creek Wildlife Management Area

Endpoints: Pittstown to · Landsdown
Location: Hunterdon County
Length: 3 miles
Surface: Original ballast

 with permit only

Contact:
Steve Smyser
Clinton Wildlife Management Area
RD 3, Box 409
Hampton, NJ 08827
908-735-8793

❹ Delaware and Raritan Canal State Park Multi-Use Trail

Endpoints: Ewing to Milford and New Brunswick to Trenton
Location: Hunterdon, Mercer and Somerset Counties
Length: 28 miles of 72-mile trail is on abandoned rail corridor
Surface: Crushed stone and gravel

on certain sections

Contact:
Paul Stern, Superintendent
Delaware and Raritan Canal State Park
643 Canal Road
Somerset, NJ 08873
908-873-3050

❺ Edgar Felix Memorial Bikeway

Endpoints: Manasquan to Allaire State Park
Location: Monmouth County
Length: 3.6 miles
Surface: Asphalt

Contact:
Thomas B. White, Director
Wall Township Parks and Recreation
2700 Allaire Road
Wall, NJ 07719
908-449-8444 Ext. 250

❻ Hamburg Mountain Wildlife Management Area Trail

Endpoints: Ogdensburg to Franklin
Location: Sussex County
Length: 5 miles
Surface: Cinder

 with permit only

Contact:
Joseph M. Penkala
Regional Superintendent
New Jersey Fish, Game and Wildlife
RD 9 Box 9126
Newton, NJ 07860

7 Henry Hudson Trail

Endpoints: Aberdeen to Atlantic Highlands
Location: Monmouth County
Length: 6 miles open in five separate sections (will be 9 miles when completed)
Surface: Dirt and cinder

Contact:
Faith Hahn, Supervising Planner
Monmouth County Park System
Newman Springs Road
Lincroft, NJ 07738
908-842-4000

8 Linwood Bikepath

Endpoints: City of Linwood
Location: Atlantic County
Length: 1.3 miles
Surface: Asphalt

Contact:
Mary Boileau, City Clerk
Linwood City Hall
400 Poplar Avenue
Linwood, NJ 08221
609-927-4108

9 Monroe Township Bikepath

Endpoints: Williamstown
Location: Gloucester County
Length: 1.5 miles
Surface: Asphalt

Contact:
Allison J. Munch
Community Affairs Director
Department of Parks
and Recreation
Monroe Township
3rd Floor, Town Hall
125 Virginia Avenue
Williamstown, NJ 08094
609-728-9823

10 Patriots Path

Endpoints: Morristown to Mendham Township
Location: Morris County
Length: 7 miles of 12-mile trail are on abandoned rail line
Surface: Cinder

Contact:
Al Kent
Morris County Park Commision
Box 1295
Morristown, NJ 07962
201-326-7600

⑪ Pequest Wildlife Management Area Trail

Endpoints: Pequest
Location: Warren County
Length: 4 miles
Surface: Original ballast

Contact:
Jim Munson, Crew Supervisor
Black River Wildlife
Management Area
Box 52, North Road
Chester, NJ 07930
908-879-6252

⑫ Sussex Branch Railroad Trail

Endpoints: Branchville to
Andover
Location: Sussex County
Length: 2.6 miles developed
near Newton (will be 13 miles
when completed)
Surface: Original ballast

Contact:
Steve Ellis, Superintendent
Swartswood State Park
P.O. Box 123
Swartswood, NJ 07877-0123
201-383-5230

⑬ Traction Line Recreation Trail

Endpoints: Morristown
Location: Morris County
Length: 2 miles
Surface: Asphalt

Contact:
Albert Kent
Patriots' Path Coordinator
Morris County Park
Commission
53 East Hanover Avenue
Box 1295
Morristown, NJ 07962-1295
201-326-7600

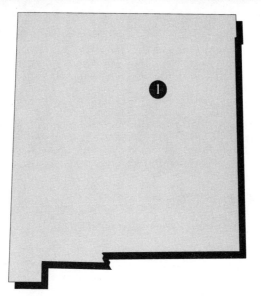

❶ *Gillinas Hiking Trail*

Endpoints: Las Vegas
Location: San Miguel County
Length: 1.5 miles (will be 7 miles when completed)
Surface: Asphalt and dirt

Contact:
Dianne Ross
Grants Administrator
City of Las Vegas
P.O. Box 179
Las Vegas, NM 87701
505-454-1401

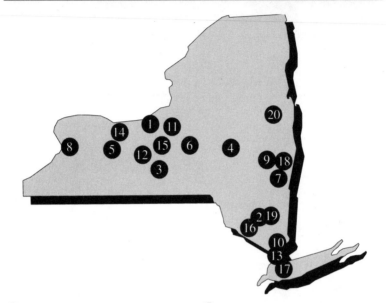

❶ *Cayuga County Trail*

Endpoints: Cato to Fair Haven
Location: Cayuga County
Length: 15 miles
Surface: Hard-packed cinder

Contact:
Tom Higgins
Cayuga County Planning Board
160 Genesee
Auburn, NY 13021
315-253-1276

❷ *D&H Canal Heritage Corridor*

Endpoints: Kingston to Port Jervis
Location: Ulster, Sullivan and Orange Counties
Length: 24 miles developed (will be 90 miles when completed, 55 miles on abandoned rail line)
Surface: Cinder

Contacts:
Rich White-Smith
New York Parks and
Conservation Association
35 Maiden Lane
Albany, NY 12207
518-434-1583

(continued)

94

JoEllen Donnelly
D&H Heritage Corridor Alliance
P.O. Box 176
Rosendale, NY 12472
914-338-5181

❸ *East Ithaca Recreation Way*

Endpoints: Town of Ithaca
Location: Tompkins County
Length: 2 miles
Surface: Crushed stone and asphalt

Contact:
Richard H. Schoch, Manager
Ithaca Parks and Open Space
106 Seven Mile Drive
Ithaca, NY 14850
607-273-8035

❹ *Erie Canal Trail*

Endpoints: Rotterdam Junction
to Oneida Lake
Location: Schenectady,
Montgomery, Herkimer and
Oneida Counties
Length: 7.5 miles developed
between Amsterdam and
Schoharie Crossing State Park
(will be 90 miles when
completed, 55 miles on
abandoned rail line)
Surface: Asphalt

Contact:
Janice Fontanella
Site Manager
Schoharie Crossing State
Historic Site
P.O. Box 140
Fort Hunter, NY 12069
518-829-7516

❺ *Genessee Valley Greenway*

Endpoints: Rochester to
Portageville
Location: Monroe and
Livingston Counties
Length: 2 miles developed in
the Village of Mount Morris (7
miles will be completed by end
of 1992, will be 50 miles when
completed)
Surface: Cinder

Contacts:
Robin Dropkin
Conservation Director
New York Parks and
Conservation Association
35 Maiden Lane
Albany, NY 12207
518-434-1583

Fran Gotshik
Local Greenway Coordinator
New York Parks and
Conservation Association
46 Prince Street
Rochester, NY 14607
716-271-3550

6 Gorge Trail

Endpoints: City of Cazenovia
Location: Madison County
Length: 2.2 miles
Surface: Original ballast and
crushed stone

Contact:
Thomas F. Vogt
Stewardship Chair
Cazenovia Preservation
Foundation
Box 432
Cazenovia, NY 13035
315-655-2397

7 Kinderhook Trail

Endpoints: Town of Kinderhook
Location: Columbia County
Length: 1 mile (will be 8 miles
when completed)
Surface: Original ballast

Contacts:
Town Recreation Commission
Box P
Niverville, NY 12130
518-758-9754

Jim Tansey
Chairman of Kinderhook Rails-
to-Trails
RD 1
Valatie, NY 12184

8 Lehigh Memory Trail

Endpoints: Williamsville
Location: Erie County
Length: .71 miles
Surface: Asphalt

Contact:
Williamsville Village Hall
5565 Main Steet
Williamsville, NY 14221
716-632-4120

⑨ Mohawk-Hudson Bikeway

Endpoints: Albany to Rotterdam Junction
Location: Albany and Schenectady Counties
Length: 19.5 miles of 41-mile trail is on abandoned rail line
Surface: Asphalt and crushed stone

Albany Section

Contact:
Albany County Planning Department
1 Lodge Street
Albany, NY 12207
518-447-5660

Colonie Section

Contact:
James G. Zambardino
Superintendent
Colonie Recreation and Parks Department
Box 442, RD 1
Cohoes, NY 12047
518-783-2760

Niskayuna Section

on certain sections

Contacts:
Elizabeth Orzel-Kaspar
Chairperson
Recreation Committee
Town of Niskayuna
1335 Balltown Road
Schenectady, NY 12309
518-374-7871

Edwin D. Reilly, Supervisor
Town of Niskayuna
1335 Balltown Road
Schenectady, NY 12309
518-374-7710

Schenectady Section

Contact:
William Seber, Director
Department of Parks and Recreation
City Hall
Jay Street
Schenectady, NY 12305
518-382-5152

Rotterdam Section

on certain sections

Contact:
Denise Cahsmere
Senior Planner
Schenectady County
Planning Department
1 Broadway Center, Suite 800
Schenectady, NY 12305-2583
518-386-2225

⑩ North County Trailway

Endpoints: Eastview to Hawthorne, Briarcliff to Law Memorial Park, Briarcliff Manor to Millwood and Mt. Pleasant to Kitchawan
Location: Westchester County
Length: 10 miles
Surface: Asphalt

Contact:
Director of Park Facilities
Westchester County
Department of Parks,
Recreation and Conservation
19 Bradhurst Avenue
Hawthorne, NY 10532
914-285-7275

⑪ Oswego Recreational Trail

Endpoints: Fulton to Constantia
Location: Oswego County
Length: 26 miles
Surface: Original ballast

Contact:
Darrell Kehoe, Crew leader
Oswego County Highway
Department
46 East Bridge Street
Oswego, NY 13126
315-349-8331

⑫ Outlet Trail

Endpoints: Dresden to Penn Yan
Location: Yates County
Length: 7.5 miles
Surface: Original ballast and asphalt

on certain sections

Contact:
Virginia H. Gibbs
County Historian
110 Court Street
Penn Yan, NY 14527
315-536-5147

⑬ Raymond Esposito Trail

Endpoints: Village of South Nyack
Location: Rockland County
Length: 1 mile
Surface: Crushed stone

Contact:
Mary Martini, Village Clerk
Village Hall
282 S. Broadway
Village of South Nyack
914-358-0287

⑭ Rochester, Syracuse and Eastern Trail

Endpoints: Town of Perinton
Location: Monroe County
Length: 5 miles (will be 8 miles when completed)
Surface: Crushed stone

Contact:
David R. Morgan
Director of Parks
1350 Turk Hill Road
Fairport, NY 14450
716-223-5050

⑮ Skaneateles Nature Trail

Endpoints: Skaneateles
Location: Onondaga County
Length: 2 miles
Surface: Dirt

Contact:
Matthew Major
Recreation Supervisor
24 Jordon Street
Skaneateles, New York 13152
315-685-6726

⑯ Sullivan County Rail-Trail

Endpoints: Westbrookville to Wurtsboro and Mountaindale to Woodridge
Location: Sullivan County
Length: 14 miles
Surface: Gravel and dirt

on certain sections
The trail is closed for hunting season starting Nov. 1 for six weeks

Contact:
Peter Rhulen
Sullivan County Rails-to-Trails Conservancy Inc.
217 Broadway
Monticello, NY 12701
914-794-8000 Ext. 222

⑰ The John Kieran Nature Trail

Endpoints: Bronx, New York City
Location: New York County
Length: .33 mile of 1-mile trail is on abandoned rail line
Surface: Original ballast and dirt

Contact:
Marianne Anderson
Van Cortlandt and Pelham Bay Parks Administration
Bronx River Parkway
Bronx, NY 10462
212-430-1890

⓲ Uncle Sam Bikeway

Endpoints: City of Troy
Location: Rensselaer County
Length: 3.8 miles
Surface: Asphalt

Contact:
Robert J. Weaver
Commissioner
Troy Parks and Recreation
Department
1 Monument Square
Troy, NY 12180
518-270-4600

⓳ Wallkill Valley Rail Trail

Endpoints: Springtown to Gardiner
Location: Ulster County
Length: 8.7 miles
Surface: Original ballast

Contact:
Roland Bahret
Wallkill Valley Rail-Trail
Association, Inc.
P.O. Box 1048
New Paltz, NY 12561
914-255-1436

⓴ Warren County Bikeway

Endpoints: Lake George to Glens Falls
Location: Warren County
Length: 10 miles
Surface: Asphalt

Contact:
Patrick Beland, Director
Warren County Parks and
Recreation Department
261 Main Street
Warrensburg, NY 12885
518-623-2877

NORTH CAROLINA

❶ Libba Cotton Trail

Endpoints: Carrboro
Location: Orange County
Length: .5 mile
Surface: Asphalt

Contact:
Roy Williford
Planning and Economic
Development Coordinator
P.O. Box 829
Carrboro, NC 27510
919-968-7714

❷ River to Sea Bikeway

Endpoints: Wilmington to
Wrightsville Beach
Location: New Hanover County
Length: 8 miles
Surface: Asphalt and concrete

Contact:
Joseph Huegy
Transportation Planner
City of Wilmington
P.O. Box 1810
Wilmington, NC 28402
919-341-7888

❸ Strollway

Endpoints: Winston-Salem
Location: Forsyth County
Length: 1.2 miles
Surface: Crushed stone

Contact:
Jack Steelman
Winston-Salem Development
Office
P.O. Box 2511
Winston-Salem, NC 27102
919-727-2741

NORTH DAKOTA

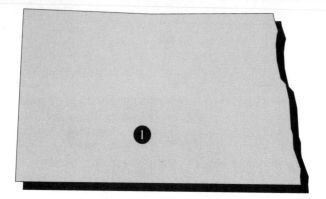

❶ *Roughrider Trail*

Endpoints: Fort Lincoln to Fort Rice
Location: Morton County
Length: 17 miles of 22-mile trail is on abandoned rail line
Surface: Dirt and gravel

Contact:
Steve Thilmony
Snowmobile and ATV
Recreation Administrator
Snowmobile North Dakota
1835 Bismarck Expressway
Bismarck, ND 58504
701-224-2525

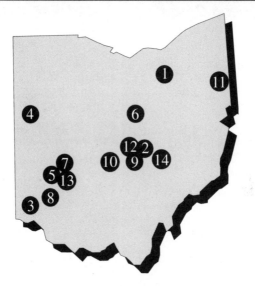

❶ Akron/Bike and Hike Trail

Endpoints: Walton Hills to Kent and Stow
Location: Cuyahoga, Summit and Portage Counties
Length: 29 miles (3 miles on-street from Silver Lake to Stow)
Surface: Asphalt and crushed stone

Akron Metro Parks, serving Summit County section

Contact:
John R. Daily, Director
Akron Metropolitan Park District
975 Treaty Line Road
Akron, OH 44313
216-867-5511

Cleveland Metroparks Section

Contact:
Steve Coles, Chief of Planning
Cleveland Metroparks
4101 Fulton Parkway
Cleveland, OH 44144
216-351-6300 ext. 238

❷ Blackhand Gorge Bikeway

Endpoints: Blackhand Gorge Nature Preserve near Toboso
Location: Licking County
Length: 4 miles
Surface: Asphalt

Contact:
William Daehler, Administrator
Comprehensive Planning Section
Division of Natural Areas and Preserves
Ohio Department of Natural Resources
Fountain Square
Columbus, OH 43224
614-265-6395

❸ California Junction Trail

Endpoints: California Woods Nature Preserve
Location: Hamilton County
Length: 1 mile
Surface: Original ballast and wood chips

Contact:
Jim Farsing
California Woods
Outdoor Recreation Center
5400 Kellogg Avenue
Cincinnati, OH 45228
513-231-8678

❹ Celina-Coldwater Bikeway

Endpoints: Celina to Coldwater
Location: Mercer County
Length: 4.6 miles
Surface: Asphalt

Contact:
Mike Sovinski
Celina Engineering Department
426 West Market
Celina, OH 45822
419-586-1144

❺ Huffman Prairie Overlook Trail

Endpoints: Bath Township
Location: Greene County
Length: 3 miles (will be 5.5 when completed)
Surface: Grass

Contact:
Elwood J. Ensor
Miami Valley Regional Bicycle Committee
1304 Horizon Drive
Fairborn, OH 45324-5816
513-879-2068
513-255-4097

⑥ Kokosing Gap Trail

Endpoints: Mt. Vernon to Danville
Location: Knox County
Length: 4.2 miles developed between Mt. Vernon and Gambier (will be 9 miles when completed)
Surface: Asphalt

Contact:
Phil Samuell
President of the Board of Directors
Kokosing Gap Trail
P.O. Box 129
Gambier, OH 43022
614-427-4509
614-587-6267

⑦ Little Miami Bike Route

Endpoints: City of Springfield
Location: Clark County
Length: 1.5 miles of 3-mile trail is on abandoned rail line
Surface: Asphalt

Contact:
Tim Smith, Director
Springfield Parks
and Recreation
City Hall
76 East High Street
Springfield, OH 45502
513-324-7348

⑧ Little Miami Scenic State Park

Endpoints: Kroger Hill to Spring Valley
Location: Greene, Warren, Clermont and Hamilton Counties
Length: 45 miles
Surface: Asphalt with parallel grass treadway (Milford to Morrow) and original ballast

 on certain sections

Contact:
Chuck Thiemann, Manager
Little Miami Scenic State Park
8570 East S.R. 73
Waynesville, OH 45068
513-897-3055 ·

⑨ Ohio Canal Greenway

Endpoints: Hebron to Licking County line
Location: Licking County
Length: 2.8 miles
Surface: Crushed limestone

Contact:
Russ Edgington
Licking Park District
4309 Lancaster Road
Granville, OH 43023
614-587-2535

⑩ Scioto Bike Path

Endpoints: Columbus
Location: Franklin County
Length: 1.5 miles of 4.75 mile-trail on abandoned rail line
Surface: Asphalt

Contact:
Mollie O'Donnell, Landscape Architect
City of Columbus Recreation and Parks Department
420 W. Whittier Street
Columbus, OH 43215
614-645-3300

⑪ Stavich Bicycle Trail

Endpoints: Struthers to New Castle, PA
Location: Mahoning County and Lawrence County, PA
Length: 12 miles
Surface: Asphalt

Contact:
Gary Slaven
Falcon Foundry
6th and Water Streets
P.O. Box 301
Lowellville, OH 44436-0301
216-536-6221

⑫ Thomas J. Evans Bike Trail

Endpoints: Newark to Johnstown
Location: Licking County
Length: 14.5 miles
Surface: Asphalt

Contact:
The Thomas J. Evans Foundation
P.O. Box 4212
Newark, OH 43055
614-345-9711

⑬ Xenia to Yellow Springs Bikeway

Endpoints: Xenia to Yellow Springs
Location: Greene County
Length: 9.7 miles
Surface: Asphalt

Contact:
Charles E. Dressler
Greene County Park District
651 Dayton-Xenia Road
Xenia, OH 45385
513-376-7440

⑭ *Zanesville Riverfront Bikepath*

Endpoints: City of Zanesville
Location: Muskingum County
Length: 2.9 miles
Surface: Asphalt

Contact:
Ernie Bynum
Recreation Director
City of Zanesville
401 Market Street
Zanesville, OH 43701
614-455-0609

OKLAHOMA

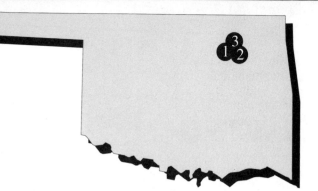

❶ *Cleveland Trail*

Endpoints: City of Cleveland
Location: Pawnee County
Length: 3 miles
Surface: Asphalt

Contact:
Larry Hall, City Manager
105 North Division
Cleveland, OK 74020
918-358-3600

❷ *Katy Trail*

Endpoints: Tulsa to Sand Springs
Location: Tulsa County
Length: 8 miles
Surface: Asphalt

Contact:
Jackie Bubenik
Executive Director
River Parks Authority
707 South Houston, Suite 202
Tulsa, OK 74127
918-596-2001

❸ *Midland Valley Trail & River Parks Pedestrian bRRridge*

Endpoints: City of Tulsa
Location: Tulsa County
Length: 1.25 miles (will be 2.25 miles when complete)
Surface: Asphalt

Contact:
Jackie Bubenik
Executive Director
River Parks Authority
707 South Houston, Suite 202
Tulsa, OK 74127
918-596-2001

OREGON

❶ *Banks-Vernonia Linear Park*

Endpoints: Banks to Vernonia
Location: Columbia County
Length: 6.5 miles (will be 18.5 miles when completed)
Surface: Gravel

Contact:
Oregon State Park
Headquarters
525 Trade Street SE
Salem, OR 97310
503-378-6305

❷ *Malheur Trail*

Endpoints: Malheur
National Forest, Murray Camp
to Summit Prairie
Location: Grant County
Length: 12.5 miles
Surface: Original ballast

Contact:
Ivan Molder, Trail Manager
139 N.E. Dayton Street
John Day, OR 97845
503-575-1731

❸ Springwater Trail Corridor

Endpoints: Gresham to Portland
Location: Multnomah and Clackamas Counties
Length: 4.8 miles developed in Gresham (will be 16.5 miles when completed)
Surface: Asphalt and gravel with parallel dirt treadway

 on certain sections

Contact:
Phil Kidby, Landscape Architect
Gresham Parks and Recreation Division
Department of Environmental Services
1333 N.W. Eastman Parkway
Gresham, OR 97030
503-669-2530

❹ Sumpter Valley Interpretive Trail

Endpoints: Malheur National Forest
Location: Grant County
Length: .2 miles
Surface: Asphalt

Contact:
Ivan Mulder, Trail Manager
Malheur National Forest
Recreation Unit
U.S. Forest Service
139 NE Dayton Street
John Day, OR 97845
503-575-1731

PENNSYLVANIA

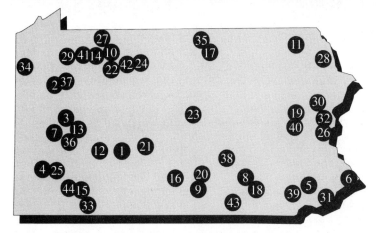

❶ Allegheny Portage Railroad Trails

Endpoints: Allegheny Portage Railroad National Historic Site
Location: Blair and Cambria Counties
Length: 7 miles
Surface: Original ballast and grass

 on certain sections

Contact:
Peter Nigh, Superintendent
Allegheny Portage Railroad
National Historic Site
P.O. Box 189
Cresson, PA 16630
814-886-6150

❷ Allegheny River Trail

Endpoints: Franklin to Brandon
Location: Venango County
Length: 14 miles
Surface: Asphalt and original ballast

 on certain sections

Contact:
Franklin Area Chamber of Commerce
1256 Liberty Street, Suite 2
Franklin, PA 16323
814-432-5823

❸ *The Armstrong Trail*

Endpoints: Schenley to Upper Hillville
Location: Armstrong and Clarion Counties
Length: 48 miles
Surface: Original ballast

Contact:
Susan Torrence
Armstrong County Tourist Bureau
402 East Market Street
Kittaning, PA 16201
412-548-3226

❹ *Arrowhead Trail*

Endpoints: Town of McMurray
Location: Washington County
Length: 3.5 miles (will be 6 miles when completed)
Surface: Asphalt and original ballast

on certain sections

Contact:
Joanne F. Nelson, Director
Peters Township Department of Parks and Recreation
610 East McMurray Road
McMurray, PA 15317
412-942-5000

❺ *Betzwood Rail Trail*

Endpoints: Valley Forge National Historic Park
Location: Montgomery County
Length: 2 miles
Surface: Original ballast

Contact:
Scott Kalbach
Chief Park Ranger
Valley Forge National Historic Park
Box 953
Valley Forge, PA 19481
215-783-1045

❻ *Bristol Spurline Park*

Endpoints: Borough of Bristol
Location: Bucks County
Length: 1 mile (will be 2 miles when completed)
Surface: Asphalt

Contact:
Fidel Esposito, Manger, or Maria Fields, Administrative Assistant
Borough of Bristol
250 Pond Street
Bristol, PA 19007
215-788-3828

7 Butler-Freeport Community Trail

Endpoints: Butler to Freeport
Location: Butler County
Length: 3 miles (will be 20 miles when completed)
Surface: Dirt and gravel

Contact:
Ron Bennett, President
Butler-Freeport Community
Trail Council
P.O. Box 533
Saxonburg, PA 16056
412-352-4783

8 Conewago Trail

Endpoints: Elizabethtown to
Lebanon County line
Location: Lancaster County
Length: 5 miles
Surface: Original ballast

Contact:
John Gerencser
Recreation Coordinator
Lancaster County
Parks and Recreation
1050 Rockford Road
Lancaster, PA 17602
717-299-8215

9 Cumberland County Biker/Hiker Trail

Endpoints: Pine Grove Furnace
State Park to Mountain Creek
Campground
Location: Cumberland County
Length: 5.5 miles
Surface: Crushed stone

Contact:
Bill Rosevear
Park Superintendent
Pine Grove Furnace State Park
RR 2, Box 399B
Gardeners, PA 17324
717-486-7174

10 Deerlick Cross-Country Ski Trail

Endpoints: Allegheny National
Forest
Location: Warren County
Length: 2 miles of 9-mile trail is
on abandoned rail line
Surface: Original ballast

Contact:
Karen Mollander
District Ranger
Sheffield Ranger District
Route 6
Sheffield, PA 16347
814-968-3232

⑪ Endless Mountain Riding Trail

Endpoints: Alford to Montrose
Location: Susquehanna County
Length: 14 miles
Surface: Original ballast

Contact:
Niki Mack, President
Bridgewater Riding Club
P.O. Box 21
Montrose, PA 18843
717-278-1318

⑫ Ghost Town Trail

Endpoints: Nanty Glo to Dilltown
Location: Cambria and Indiana Counties
Length: 12 miles, (will be 19.5 when completed)
Surface: Original ballast

Contact:
Ed Patterson
Indiana County Parks
RD 2, Box 157-J
Indiana, PA 15701
412-463-8636

⑬ Great Shamokin Path

Endpoints: Yatesboro to NuMine
Location: Armstrong County
Length: 4 miles
Surface: Gravel and original ballast

Contact:
Pam Meade, President
Cowanshannock Creek
Watershed Association
P.O. Box 307
Rural Valley, PA 16249
412-783-6692

⑭ Heart's Content Cross-Country Ski Trail

Endpoints: Allegheny National Forest
Location: Warren County
Heart's Content Recreation Area
Length: 3.7 miles of 7.7-mile trail is on abandoned rail line
Surface: Original ballast

Contact:
Karen Mollander
District Ranger
Sheffield Ranger District
Route 6
Sheffield, PA 16347
814-968-3232

15 Indian Creek Valley Hiking and Biking Trail

Endpoints: C.W. Resch Memorial Park to Springfield
Location: Fayette and Westmoreland Counties
Length: 5 miles developed in Salt Lick Township (will be 23 miles when completed)
Surface: Original ballast

Contact:
Evelyn Dix, Secretary
Salt Lick Township
P.O. Box 403
Melcroft, PA 15462
412-455-2866

16 Iron Horse Trail

Endpoints: Big Spring State Park to southwest of New Germantown
Location: Perry County
Length: 10 miles
Surface: Dirt and original ballast

Contact:
Ernie Geanette
Bureau of Forestry
RD 1, Box 42A
Blain, PA 17006
717-536-3191

17 Lambs Creek Hike and Bike Trail

Endpoints: Mansfield to Lambs Creek Recreation Area
Location: Tioga County
Length: 3.2 miles
Surface: Asphalt

Contact:
Richard J. Koeppel
Park Manager
U.S. Army Corps of Engineers
RD 1, Box 65
Tioga, PA 16946
717-835-5281

18 Lancaster Junction Trail

Endpoints: Lancaster Junction to Landisville
Location: Lancaster County
Length: 2.5 miles
Surface: Original ballast

Contact:
John Gerencser
Recreation Coordinator
Lancaster County
Parks and Recreation
1050 Rockford Road
Lancaster, PA 17602
717-299-8215

⑲ Lehigh Gorge State Park Trail

Endpoints: White Haven to Jim Thorpe
Location: Luzerne and Carbon Counties
Length: 25 miles
Surface: Original ballast and crushed stone

 on certain sections

Contact:
Kevin Fazzine
Park Superintendent
Lehigh Gorge State Park
RD 2, Box 56
Weatherly, PA 18255
717-427-8161

⑳ LeTort Spring Run Nature Trail

Endpoints: Carlisle to South Middleton Township
Location: Cumberland County
Length: 1.4 miles
Surface: Original ballast

Contact:
Kenwood Giffhorn
Executive Director
LeTort Regional Authority
415 Franklin Street
Carlisle, PA 17013
717-249-6139

㉑ Lower Trail

Endpoints: Alexandria to Williamsburg
Location: Blair and Huntingdon Counties
Length: 11 miles
Surface: Original ballast

Contact:
Palmer Brown, President
or Jennifer Barefoot
Rails-to-Trails
of Blair County, Inc.
221 High Street
Williamsburg, PA 16693
814-832-2400

㉒ Marienville ATV/ Bike Trail

Endpoints: Allegheny National Forest, treailhead on Route 66, 11 miles north of Marienville
Location: Forest and Elk Counties
Length: 3.8 miles of 36-mile system is on abandoned rail line
Surface: Original ballast

Contact:
Theodore Beauvais
District Ranger
Marienville Ranger District
Marienville, PA 16347
814-927-6628

㉓ Mid State Trail, Penns Creek Section

Endpoints: Poe Paddy State Park to Cherry Run
Location: Centre, Mifflin and Snyder Counties
Length: 3.2 miles of 206-mile trail is on abandoned rail line
Surface: Original ballast

 on certain sections

Contact:
Thomas T. Thwaites, President
Mid State Trail Association
P.O. Box 167
Boalsburg, PA 16827
814-237-7703

㉔ Mill Creek Loop Trail

Endpoints: Allegheny National Forest, Twin Lakes Recreation Area
Location: Elk County
Length: 3.1 miles of 16.7-mile trail is on abandoned rail line
Surface: Original ballast

Contact:
Leon Blashock
District Ranger
Ridgway Ranger District
RD 1, Box 28A
Ridgway, PA 15853
814-776-6172

㉕ Montour Trail

Endpoints: Coraopolis to Clairton
Location: Allegheny and Washington Counties
Length: 4.4 miles developed between Cecil Park and Hendersonville (will be 55 miles when completed)
Surface: Crushed limestone with parallel dirt treadway

Contact:
Tom Fix
The Montour Trail Council
P.O. Box 11866
Pittsburgh, PA 15228-0866
412-831-2030

㉖ National Trails Towpath Bike Trail of Palmer and Bethlehem Townships

Endpoints: Palmer to Bethlehem
Location: Northampton County
Length: 7.8 miles
Surface: Asphalt

Contact:
H. Robert Daws, Chairman
Palmer Township Board of Supervisors
P.O. Box 3039
Palmer, PA 18043
215-253-7191

㉗ North Country National Scenic Trail (Allegheny National Forest Section)

Endpoints: Warren to New York state line
Location: Warren County
Length: 6.8 miles of 86.8-mile trail is on abandoned rail line
Surface: Original ballast

Contact:
Forest Supervisor
222 Liberty Avenue
Warren, PA 16365
814-723-5150

㉘ O&W Road Trail

Endpoints: Preston Township line to Delaware River
Location: Wayne and Susquehanna Counties
Length: 6 miles (will be 32 miles when completed)
Surface: Cinder

Contact:
Phil Pass
Rail Trail Council of Northeast Pennsylvania
P.O. Box 100
Clifford, PA 18413
717-222-3333

㉙ Oil Creek State Park Trail

Endpoints: Petroleum Centre to Drake Well Museum near Titusville
Location: Crawford and Venango Counties
Length: 9.7 miles
Surface: Asphalt

Contact:
Nick Kerlin, Park Manager
Oil Creek State Park
RR 1, Box 207
Oil City, PA 16301
814-676-5915

㉚ Old Railroad Trail

Endpoints: Big Pocono State Park to Crescent Lake
Location: Monroe County
Length: 8.4 miles
Surface: Original ballast

Contact:
Ronald Dixon
Big Pocono State Park
c/o Tobyhanna State Park
Box 387
Tobyhanna, PA 18466
717-894-8336

31 Philadelphia to Valley Forge Bikeway

Endpoints: Philadelphia to Valley Forge
Location: Philadelphia and Montgomery Counties
Length: 11.5 miles of 21-mile trail is on abandoned rail line
Surface: Asphalt and original ballast

 on certain sections

Contact:
John H. Wood
Chief of Open Space Planning
Montgomery County Planning
Commission
Court House
Norristown, PA 19404
215-278-3736

32 Plainfield Township Trail

Endpoints: Plainfield Township
Location: Northampton County
Length: 6.7 miles
Surface: Asphalt

Contact:
Anita Bray
Supervisor/Secretary
Plainfield Board of Supervisors
517 Getz Road
Nazareth, PA 18064
215-759-6944

33 PW&S Railroad Hiking-Biking Trail

Endpoints: Forbes State Park
Location: Westmoreland and Somerset Counties
Length: 9.5 miles of 29-mile section on abandoned rail line
Surface: Dirt

Two sections within the park:
2.5-mile section

29-mile section

 on certain sections

Contact:
Lysle S. Sherwin
Executive Director
Loyalhanna Watershed
Association
P.O. Box 561
Ligonier, PA 15658
412-238-7560

34 Pymatuning State Park Trail

Endpoints: Pymatuning State Park
Location: Crawford County
Length: 1.7 miles
Surface: Original ballast

Contact:
Eugene Hart, Park Manager
Pymatuning State Park
P.O. Box 425
Jamestown, PA 16134
412-932-3141

35 Railroad Grade Trail

Endpoints: Ives Run Recreation Area to Hills Creek Road
Location: Tioga County
Length: 2.6 miles
Surface: Original ballast

Trail is open to automobile traffic from mid-April through Memorial Day and October through December

Contact:
R.J. Koeppel
Park Manager
U.S. Army Corps of Engineers
RD 1, Box 65
Tioga, PA 16946-9733
717-835-5281

36 Roaring Run Trail

Endpoints: Kiskiminetas Township
Location: Armstrong County
Length: 1.5 miles
Surface: Crushed limestone

Contact:
Andy Schreffler, Director
Roaring Run Watershed Association
215 Rovel Street
Apollo, PA 15613
412-568-1483

37 Samuel Justus Recreational Trail

Endpoints: Franklin to Oil City
Location: Venango County
Length: 5.8 miles
Surface: Asphalt

Contact:
Richard A. Castonguay
Secretary
Cranberry Township
P.O. Box 378
Seneca, PA 16346
814-676-8812

㉘ Stony Valley Railroad Grade

Endpoints: Dauphin to Lebanon Reservoir
Location: Dauphin, Lebanon and Schuylkill Counties
Length: 22 miles
Surface: Crushed stone

Contact:
Roger L. Lehman, Chief
Federal-State Coordination Division
Pennsylvania Game Commission
2001 Elmerton Avenue
Harrisburg, PA 17100-9797
717-787-9612

㉙ Struble Trail

Endpoints: Downingtown to Honeybrook
Location: Chester County
Length: 5 miles developed from Downingtown to Uwchlan Township (will be 16 miles when completed)
Surface: Asphalt

Contact:
Robert Folwell
Chester County Parks and Recreation Department
235 West Market Street
West Chester, PA 19382
215-344-6415

㉛ Switchback Railroad Trail

Endpoints: Summit Hill to Jim Thorpe
Location: Carbon County
Length: 15 miles
Surface: Original ballast

Contact:
Dennis J. DeMara
Park Director
Carbon County Park and Recreation Department
625 Lentz Trail Road
Jim Thorpe, PA 18229
717-325-3669

㉜ Tidioute Riverside RecTrek Trail

Endpoints: Allegheny National Forest, Tidioute to National Forest Lands System
Location: Warren County
Length: 2.5 miles
Surface: Original ballast and grass

Contact:
Karen Mollander
District Ranger
Sheffield Ranger District
Route 6
Sheffield, PA 16347
814-968-3232

㊷ Twin Lakes Trail

Endpoints: Allegheny
National Forest, Twin Lakes
Recreation Area to North
Country National Scenic Trail
Location: Elk and Forest
Counties
Length: 1.3 miles of 14.7-mile
trail is on abandoned rail line
Surface: Original ballast

Contact:
Leon Blashock
District Ranger
Ridgway Ranger District
RD 1, Box 28A
Ridgway, PA 15853
814-776-6172

㊸ York County Heritage Rail-Trail

Endpoints: Spring Garden
Township to Maryland state line
Location: York County
Length: 1.5 miles open in early
1993 between New Freedom
and Maryland state line (will be
22 miles when completed)
Surface: Crushed stone

Contact:
Tammy Klunk
Resource Coordinator
York County Parks
400 Mundis Race Road
York, PA 17402
717-771-9440

㊹ Youghiogheny River Trail

Endpoints: Confluence to
McKeesport
Location: Fayette, Somerset,
Westmoreland and Allegheny
Counties
Length: 69 miles
Surface: Crushed stone

Confluence-Connellsville Section

Length: 27 miles (will be 28
miles when completed)

Contact:
Douglas Hoehn
Park Superintendent
Ohiopyle State Park
P.O. Box 105
Ohiopyle, PA 15470
412-329-8591

Connellsville-McKeesport Section

Length: 15 miles in three
sections with parallel dirt
treadway scheduled to open in
early 1993 (will be 41 miles
when completed)

Contact:
Larry Ridenour, President
Regional Trail Corporation
RD 12, Box 203
Greensburg, PA 15601
412-355-5872

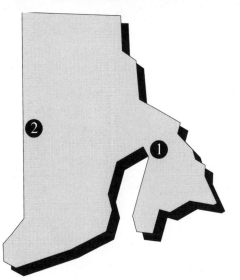

❶ *East Bay Bicycle Path*

Endpoints: Bristol to Providence
Location: Bristol County and
Greater Providence
Length: 14 miles
Surface: Asphalt

Contact:
Kevin O'Malley
Regional Manager
Colt State Park
Bristol, RI   02809
401-253-7482

❷ *Trestle Trail*

Endpoints: Coventry Center to
Connecticut state line
Location: Kent County
Length: 8 miles
Surface: Original ballast

Contact:
Ginny Leslie, Senior Planner
Rhode Island Department of
Environmental Management
Division of Planning and
Development
83 Park Street
Providence, RI   02903
401-277-2776

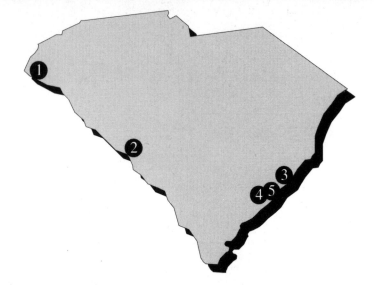

❶ *Blue Ridge Railroad Historical Trail*

Endpoints: Stumphouse Tunnel to northwest of Walhalla
Location: Oconee County
Length: 5 miles
Surface: Dirt and chipped bark

Contact:
Hurley E. Badders
Executive Director
Pendleton District
Historical and Recreational
Commission
P.O. Box 565
Pendleton, SC 29670
803-646-3782

❷ *North Augusta Trail*

Endpoints: North Augusta
Location: Aiken County
Length: 1 mile (will be 5.2 miles and paved when completed in 1993)
Surface: Dirt

when paved

Contact:
J. Robert Brooks
Director of Parks and
Recreation
P.O. Box 6400
North Augusta, S.C. 29841
803-278-2358

❸ Swamp Fox National Recreation Trail

Endpoints: Francis Marion National Forest
Location: Berkeley and Charleston Counties
Length: 6 miles of 21-mile trail is on abandoned rail line
Surface: Original ballast and sand

Contact:
Bill Craig
Recreation Staff Officer
U.S. Forest Service
1835 Assembly Street, Rm. 333
Columbia, SC 29201
803-253-3184

❹ West Ashley Bikeway

Endpoints: City of Charleston
Location: Charleston County
Length: 2 miles
Surface: Asphalt

Contact:
Kirk West
Department of Parks
30 Mary Murray Drive
Charleston, SC 29403
803-724-7321

❺ West Ashley Greenway

Endpoints: Albemarle Road to Clemson Experimental Station (parallel to Highway 17)
Location: Charleston County
Length: 7.5 miles
Surface: Dirt

on certain sections

Contact:
Kirk West
Department of Parks
30 Mary Murray Drive
Charleston, SC 29403
803-724-7321

SOUTH DAKOTA

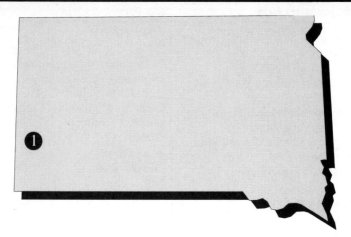

❶ *Black Hills Burlington Northern Heritage Trail*

Endpoints: Deadwood to Edgemont
Location: Lawrence and Custer Counties
Length: 6 miles developed in Lead and 3 miles developed in Custer (will be 104 miles when completed)
Surface: Gravel

on Lead section

Contact:
Dave Johnson or Kim Raap
South Dakota Game, Fish and Parks
523 E. Capitol
Pierre, SD 57501
605-773-3391

TENNESSEE

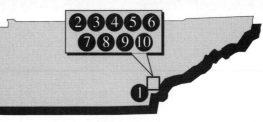

❶ Bald River Trail

Endpoints: Cherokee National Forest, Tellico Ranger District Trail #88, Bald River Falls (on FDR #210) to Bald River Road (FDR 126)
Location: Monroe County
Length: 5.6 miles
Surface: Original ballast

Contact:
Larry Fleming, District Ranger
P.O. Box 339
Tellico Plains, TN 37385
615-253-2520

❷ Conasauga River Trail

Endpoints: Cherokee National Forest, FDR 221
Location: Polk County
Length: 2.5 miles of 4.5-mile trail is on abandoned rail line
Surface: Dirt

Contact:
Larry Fleming, District Ranger
P.O. Box 339
Tellico Plains, TN 37385
615-253-2520

❸ Crowder Branch Trail

Endpoints: Cherokee National Forest, FDR 59 to FDT 95
Location: Monroe County
Length: 1.5 miles of 2.6-mile trail is on abandoned rail line
Surface: Dirt

Contact:
Larry Fleming, District Ranger
P.O. Box 339
Tellico Plains, TN 37385
615-253-2520

❹ Grassy Branch Trail

Endpoints: Cherokee National Forest, Tellico-Robinsville Road to South Fork Citico Trail
Location: Monroe County
Length: 2.7 miles of 3.2-mile trail is on abandoned rail line
Surface: Dirt

Contact:
Larry Fleming, District Ranger
P.O. Box 339
Tellico Plains, TN 37385
615-253-2520

❺ Hemlock Trail

Endpoints: Cherokee National Forest, FDR 217 to Tennessee Highway 165
Location: Monroe County
Length: 2 miles of 3-mile trail is on abandoned rail line
Surface: Dirt

Contact:
Larry Fleming, District Ranger
P.O. Box 339
Tellico Plains, TN 37385
615-253-2520

❻ Laurel Branch Trail

Endpoints: Cherokee National Forest, FDR 217 to TN 165
Location: Monroe County
Length: 2 miles of 3-mile trail is on abandoned rail line
Surface: Dirt

Contact:
Larry Fleming, District Ranger
P.O. Box 339
Tellico Plains, TN 37385
615-253-2520

❼ Long Branch Trail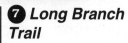

Endpoints: Cherokee National Forest, FDR 217 to TN 165
Location: Monroe County
Length: 1.5 miles of 2.7-mile trail is on abandoned rail line
Surface: Dirt

Contact:
Larry Fleming, District Ranger
P.O. Box 339
Tellico Plains, TN 37385
615-253-2520

❽ McNabb Creek Trail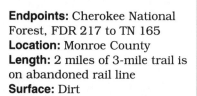

Endpoints: Cherokee National Forest, Tellico Ranger District Trail #92, Tellico-Robinsville Road at Grassy Gap to North River Road (217) near the mouth of McNabb Creek
Location: Monroe County
Length: 2 miles of 3.9-mile trail is on abandoned rail line
Surface: Original ballast

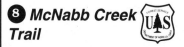

Contact:
Larry Fleming, District Ranger
P.O. Box 339
Tellico Plains, TN 37385
615-253-2520

9 North Fork Citico Trail

Endpoints: Cherokee National Forest, Tellico Ranger District Trail #98, Cherry Log Gap (off Fodderstack Trail) to North Fork Citico Road (FDR 29)
Location: Monroe County
Length: 5 miles
Surface: Original ballast

Contact:
Larry Fleming, District Ranger
P.O. Box 339
Tellico Plains, TN 37385
615-253-2520

10 South Fork Citico Trail

Endpoints: Cherokee National Forest, Tellico Ranger District, Trail #105, Strawberry Knob Road (217-H) to North Fork Citico Road (FDR29)
Location: Monroe County
Length: 7 miles of 8.1-mile trail is on abandoned rail line
Surface: Original ballast

Contact:
Larry Fleming, District Ranger
P.O. Box 339
Tellico Plains, TN 37385
615-253-2520

TEXAS

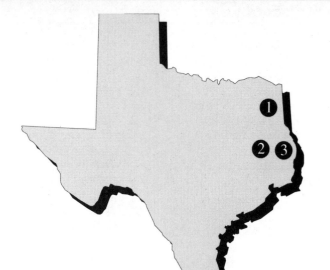

❶ *Cargill Long Park Trail*

Endpoints: Town of Longview
Location: Gregg County
Length: 2.5 miles
Surface: Asphalt

Contact:
Paul Boorman, Manager
Longview Parks and Leisure
Services
P.O. Box 1952
Longview, TX 75606
903-757-4555

❷ *Four-C Hiking Trail*

Endpoints: Davy Crockett
National Forest
Location: Houston County
Length: 20 miles
Surface: Original ballast

Contact:
Duane Strock
Landscape Architect
Department of Recreation
U.S. Forest Service
701 North 1st Street
Lufkin, TX 75901
409-639-8529

❸ Sawmill Hiking Trail

Endpoints: Angelina National Forest
Location: Angelina and Jasper Counties
Length: 5 miles
Surface: Dirt

Contact:
Catherine Albers
Resource Forester
Angelina Ranger District
1907 Atkinson Drive
Lufkin, TX 75901
409-639-8620

UTAH

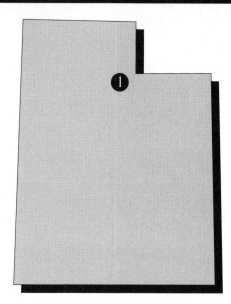

❶ *Historic Union Pacific Rail Trail*

Endpoints: Echo Junction to Park City
Location: Summit County
Length: 24 miles
Surface: Original ballast

Contact:
John Knudson
Department of Natural Resources
Division of Parks and Recreation
1636 West North Temple
Salt Lake City, UT 84116
801-538-7344

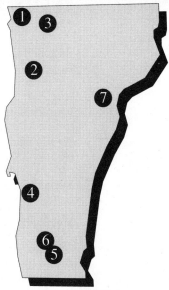

❶ *Alburg Rail-Trail*

Endpoints: Alburg to East Alburg
Location: Grand Isle County
Length: 5.1 miles
Surface: Cinder and dirt

Contact:
Trails Coordinator
Department of Forest, Parks and Recreation
111 West Street
Essex Junction, VT 05452
802-879-6565

❷ *Burlington Waterfront Bikeway*

Endpoints: City of Burlington
Location: Chittenden County
Length: 8.5 miles
Surface: Asphalt

 on certain sections

Contact:
Robert Whalen
Superintendent of Parks
Department of Parks and Recreation
216 Leddy Park Road
Burlington, VT 05401
802-864-0123

❸ *Central Vermont Trail*

Endpoints: St. Albans to Richford
Location: Franklin County
Length: 8 miles developed between St. Albans and Sheldon Junction (will be 22 miles when completed)
Surface: Original ballast

Contact:
Trails Coordinator
Department of Forest, Parks and Recreation
111 West Street
Essex Junction, VT 05452
802-879-6565

❹ *Delaware and Hudson Recreation Trail*

Endpoints: Castleton to West Rupert
Location: Bennington and Rutland Counties
Length: 20 miles developed from Castleton to Poultney and West Pawlet to West Rupert (will be 34.3 miles when completed)
Surface: Gravel and original ballast

Contact:
Gary Salmon
Trails Coordinator
Department of Forests, Parks and Recreation
Vermont Agency of Natural Resources
RD 2 Box 261
Pittsford, VT 05763
802-483-2314

❺ East Branch Trail

Endpoints: Green Mountain National Forest, Searsburg Reservoir to Somerset Reservoir
Location: Windham County
Length: 4.5 miles of 5.1-mile trail is on abandoned rail line
Surface: Gravel

Contact:
Robert M. Pramuk
Recreation Forester
P.O. Box 519
Rutland, VT 05702
802-773-0300

❻ Lye Brook Trail

Endpoints: Green Mountain National Forest, Appalachian Trail at Stratton Pond to Manchester Town Road 77
Location: Bennington and Windham Counties
Length: 4.1 miles of 9.7-mile trail is on abandoned rail line
Surface: Gravel

Contact:
Robert M. Pramuk
Recreation Forester
P.O. Box 519
Rutland, VT 05702
802-773-0300

❼ Montpelier and Wells River Trail

Endpoints: Groton State Forest
Location: Caledonia County
Length: 17 miles
Surface: Gravel and original ballast

Contact:
George Plumb
Director of Recreation
Department of Forests, Parks and Recreation
Vermont Agency of Natural Resources
103 South Main Street
Waterbury, VT 05676
802-244-8713

VIRGINIA

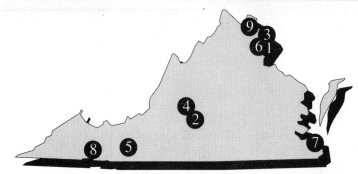

❶ *Accotink Trail*

Endpoints: Springfield
Location: Fairfax County
Length: 2.2 miles of 3.75-mile trail is on abandoned rail line
Surface: Gravel and asphalt

on certain sections

Contact:
Kirk Kincannon
Park Specialist III
Lake Accotink Park
Fairfax County Park Authority
3701 Pender Drive
Fairfax, VA 22030
703-569-0285

❷ *Blackwater Creek Natural Area Bikeway*

Endpoints: City of Lynchburg
Location: Campbell County
Length: 4 miles
Surface: Asphalt

Contact:
Chris Stinnette, Park Ranger
City of Lynchburg Recreation and Parks Department
301 Grove Street
Lynchburg, VA 24501
804-847-1640

❸ Bluemont Junction Trail

Endpoints: Arlington
Location: Arlington County
Length: 1.3 miles
Surface: Asphalt

Contact:
Ritch Viola, Planner
Arlington County
Department of Public Works
2100 Clarendon Boulevard,
Suite 717
Arlington, VA 22201
703-358-3699

❹ Chessie Nature Trail

Endpoints: Lexington to Buena
Vista
Location: Rockbridge County
Length: 7.5 miles
Surface: Crushed stone

Contact:
Louise K. Dooley
VMI Foundation
P.O. Box 932
Lexington, VA 24450
703-464-7221

❺ New River Trail State Park

Endpoints: Pulaski to Galax and
Fries
Location: Pulaski, Carroll,
Grayson and Wythe Counties
Length: 40 miles developed
from Pulaski to Allisonia and
Shot Tower to Galax and Fries
(will be 57 miles when
completed)
Surface: Original ballast

Contact:
Anthony Slate, Chief Ranger
New River Trail State Park
Route 1, Box 81X
Austinville, VA 24312
703-699-6778

❻ Orange and Alexandria Historical Trail

Endpoints: Lake Accotink Park
Location: Fairfax County
Length: 3 miles
Surface: Asphalt and crushed
stone

Contact:
Kirk Kincannon
Park Specialist III
Lake Accotink Park
Fairfax County Park Authority
3701 Pender Drive
Fairfax, VA 22030
703-569-0285

⑦ Park Connector Bikeway

Endpoints: Mt. Trashmore to Princess Anne Park
Location: Virginia Beach
Length: 4.9 miles
Surface: Asphalt

Contact:
Travis Campbell or Steve White
Department of Planning
Operations Building, Rm. 115
2405 Courthouse Drive
Virginia Beach, VA 23456
804-427-4621

⑧ Virginia Creeper National Recreation Trail

Endpoints: Abingdon to White Top
Location: Washington and Grayson Counties
Length: 34.1 miles
Surface: Original ballast

Abingdon-Damascus Section

Contact:
Tina Counts
Abingdon Convention and Visitors Bureau
208 West Main Street
Abingdon, VA 24210
703-676-2282

Damascus-White Top Section

Contact:
Area Ranger
Mt. Rogers National Recreation Area
Route 1, Box 303
Marion, VA 24354
703-783-5196

⑨ Washington and Old Dominion (W&OD) Railroad Regional Park

Endpoints: Arlington to Purcellville
Location: Arlington, Fairfax and Loudoun Counties
Length: 45 miles
Surface: Asphalt with parallel curshed stone treadway

Contact:
Paul McCray, Park Manager
Northern Virginia Regional Park Authority
5400 Ox Road
Fairfax Station, VA 22039
703-729-0596

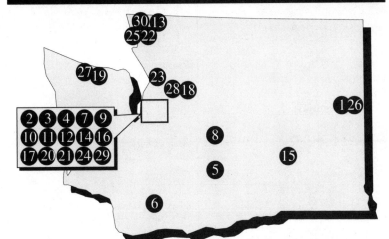

❶ *Benn Burr Trail*

Endpoints: Spokane
Location: Spokane County
Length: 1.1 miles
Surface: Dirt and gravel

Contact:
Taylor Bressler
Division Manager
City of Spokane Parks
Department
N. 809 Washington Street
Spokane, WA 99201-3317
509-625-6655

❷ *Burke-Gilman Trail*

Endpoints: Seattle to Bothell
Location: King County
Length: 16 miles developed (will
be 17 miles when completed)
Surface: Asphalt

Contacts:
Peter Lagerwey, Coordinator
Bicycle/Pedestrian Program
Seattle Engineering Department
708 Municipal Building
600 4th Avenue
Seattle, WA 98104
206-684-7583

Tom Eksten
King County Office of Open
Space
1621 Smith Tower
Seattle, WA 98104
206-296-7800

❸ City of Snoqualmie Centennial Trail

Endpoints: City of Snoqualmie
Location: King County
Length: .5 mile
Surface: Asphalt

Contact:
Leroy Gmazel
City of Snoqualmie
P.O. Box 987
Snoqualmie, WA 98065
206-888-5337

❹ Coal Creek Park Trail

Endpoints: Newcastle Road to
Meadow
Location: King County
Length: 1 mile
Surface: Original ballast and
dirt

Contact:
Tom Eksten
Trails Coordinator
King County Office of Open
Space
1621 Smith Tower
Seattle, WA 98104
206-296-7800

❺ Cowiche Canyon Trail

Endpoints: Weikel Road to
Cowiche Canyon Road
Location: Yakima County
Length: 3 miles
Surface: Dirt and gravel

Contact:
Helen Riehl, President
Cowiche Canyon Conservancy
P.O. Box 877
Yakima, WA 98907
509-966-3880

❻ Dry Creek Trail

Endpoints: Gifford Pinchot
National Forest, Junction Trail
192 to Junction Trail 158
Location: Skamania County
Length: 1.5 miles of 4-mile trail
is on abandoned rail line
Surface: Original ballast

Contact:
Dorris Tai
Trails Coordinator
Gifford Pinchot National Forest
6926 E. Fourth Plain Boulevard
P.O. Box 8944
Vancouver, WA 98668-8944
206-750-5011

7 Duwamish Bikeway

Endpoints: City of Seattle
Location: King County
Length: .75-mile of 4-mile trail
is on abandoned rail line (will
be 4.5 miles when completed)
Surface: Asphalt

Contact:
Peter Lagerwey, Coordinator
Bicycle/Pedestrian Program
Seattle Engineering Department
708 Municipal Building
600 4th Avenue
Seattle, WA 98104
206-684-7583

8 Iron Horse State Park

Endpoints: North Bend to
Vantage
Location: King and Kittitas
Counties
Length: 82 miles developed
from Hyak to Cabin Creek,
Easton to Thorp, and
Ellensburg to Vantage (will be
110 miles when completed)
Surface: Original ballast

Contact:
Iron Horse State Park
Washington State Park
and Recreation Commission
P.O. Box 26
Easton, WA 98925
509-656-2586

9 Issaquah Creek Trail

Endpoints: High Point to
Issaquah
Location: King County
Length: 2 miles
Surface: Original ballast

Contact:
Tom Eksten
Trails Coordinator
King County Office of Open
Space
1621 Smith Tower
Seattle, WA 98104
206-296-7800

10 Issaquah Trail

Endpoints: Issaquah
Location: King County
Length: 2.5 miles
Surface: Concrete and dirt

 on certain sections

Contact:
Issaquah Parks and Recreation
Department
135 E. Sunset Way
Issaquah, WA 98027
206-391-1008

⓫ King County Interurban Trail

Endpoints: Tukwila to Pacific
Location: King County
Length: 14 miles (will be 16 miles when completed)
Surface: Asphalt

 on certain sections

Contact:
Tom Eksten
King County Office of Open Space
1621 Smith Tower
Seattle, WA 98104
206-296-7800

⓬ Lake Wilderness Trail

Endpoints: Maple Valley to Lake Wilderness
Location: King County
Length: 2.7 miles
Surface: Original ballast

Contact:
Tom Eksten
King County Office of Open Space
1621 Smith Tower
Seattle, WA 98104
206-296-7800

⓭ Maple Falls to Glacier Trail

Endpoints: Maple Falls to Glacier
Location: Whatcom County
Length: 6.8 miles
Surface: Original ballast

Contact:
Roger DeSpain, Director
Whatcom County Parks and Recreation Board
3373 Mount Baker Highway
Bellingham, WA 98226
206-733-2900

⓮ Middle Fork Snoqualmie River Trail

Endpoints: Mt. Baker-Snoqualmie National Forest, North Bend Ranger District
Location: King County
Length: 5 miles of 17-mile trail is on abandoned rail line
Surface: Original ballast

Contact:
Kathy White
Forestry Technician
Mt. Baker Snoqualmie National Forest
North Bend Ranger District
42404 S.E. North Bend Way
North Bend, WA 98045
206-888-1421

⓯ Milwaukee Road Corridor

Endpoints: Columbia River near Wanapum Dam to Idaho state line near Tekoa
Location: Grant, Adams and Whitman Counties
Length: 145 miles
Surface: Original ballast
All use is by permit only

Contact:
James Munroe
Washington Department of Natural Resources
713 East Bowers Road
Ellensburg, WA 98926
509-925-6131

⓰ Myrtle Edwards Park Trail

Endpoints: City of Seattle
Location: King County
Length: 1.25 miles
Surface: Asphalt with two parallel dirt treadways

Contact:
Peter Lagerwey, Coordinator
Bicycle/Pedestrian Program
Seattle Engineering Department
708 Municipal Building
600 4th Avenue
Seattle, WA 98104
206-684-7583

⓱ Necklace Valley Trail

Endpoints: Skykomish
Location: King County
Length: 1.5 miles
Surface: Dirt

Contact:
Tom Davis, Trail Specialist
Skykomish Ranger District
P.O. Box 305
Skykomish, WA 98288
206-677-2414

⓲ Pacific Crest National Scenic Trail

Endpoints: Stevens Pass to Yodelin
Location: Chelan County
Length: 1.5 miles of the trail is on abandoned rail line
Surface: Dirt and grass

Contact:
Roger Ross
Trails and Wilderness Coordinator
U.S. Forest Service
Lake Wanache Ranger District
22976 Highway 207
Leavenworth, WA 98826
509-763-3103

⑲ Port Angeles Urban Waterfront Trail

Endpoints: Port Angeles City
Location: Clallam County
Length: 3 miles of 5-mile trail is on abandoned rail line
(will be 10 miles with 8 miles on abandoned rail line when completed)
Surface: Asphalt

Contact:
Scott Brodhun, Director
City of Port Angeles Parks and Recreation
321 East Fifth Street
Port Angeles, WA 98362
206-457-0411 Ext. 215

⑳ Preston Railroad Trail

Endpoints: Tiger Mountain State Forest (Crossover Road 5500 to Main Tiger Mountain Road 4000)
Location: King County
Length: 5 miles
Surface: Original ballast

Contact:
Doug McClelland
Issaquah Unit Forester
Tiger Mountain State Forest
P.O. Box 68
Enumclaw, WA 98022
206-825-1631

㉑ Preston-Snoqualmie Trail

Endpoints: Preston to Snoqualmie Falls
Location: King County
Length: 6.3 miles developed from Preston to near Fall City (will be 9 miles when completed)
Surface: Asphalt

Contact:
Tom Eksten
King County Office of Open Space
1621 Smith Tower
Seattle, WA 98104
206-296-7800

㉒ Railroad Trail

Endpoints: Sunnyland Memorial Park to Lake Whatcom
Location: Whatcom County
Length: 2 miles developed (will be 6.5 miles when completed, 4.2 miles on abandoned rail line)
Surface: Crushed stone

Contact:
Trail Planner
Bellingham Parks and Recreation Department
210 Lottie Street
Bellingham, WA 98225

㉓ Snohomish County Centennial Trail

Endpoints: Skagit County line to King County line
Location: Snohomish County
Length: 6 miles (will be 44 miles when completed)
Surface: Asphalt with parallel gravel path

Contact:
Mike Parman
Senior Parks Planner
Snohomish County Parks and Recreation Division
3000 Rockefeller Avenue
Everett, WA 98201
206-388-6621

㉔ Snoqualmie Valley Trail

Endpoints: Carnation to Snoqualmie Falls
Location: King County
Length: 11 miles
Surface: Original ballast

Contact:
Tom Eksten
Trails Coordinator
King County Office of Open Space
1621 Smith Tower
Seattle, WA 98104
206-296-7800

㉕ South Bay Trail

Endpoints: City of Bellingham
Location: Whatcom County
Length: 1.5 miles
Surface: Crushed stone

Contact:
Bellingham Parks and Recreation Department
210 Lottie Street
Bellingham, WA 98225

㉖ Spokane River Centennial Trail

Endpoints: Idaho state line to Spokane House
Location: Spokane County
Length: 10 miles of 32-mile trail is on abandoned rail line (will be 39 miles when completed)
Surface: Asphalt

 on certain sections

🛼 no poles

Contacts:
Friends of the Centennial Trail
P.O. Box 351
Spokane, WA 99201
509-624-3430

Gary Herron
Riverside State Park Centennial Trail Administrator
4427 Aubrey L. White Parkway
Spokane, WA 99205
509-456-2729

㉗ Spruce Railroad Trail

Endpoints: Olympic National Park, along the shores of Lake Crescent
Location: Clallam County
Length: 4 miles
Surface: Dirt and gravel

Contact:
Bill Pierce, Chief Ranger
National Park Service
Olympic National Park
600 East Park Avenue
Port Angeles, WA 98362
206-452-4501

㉘ Wallace Falls Railway Grade

Endpoints: Wallace Falls State Park
Location: Snohomish County
Length: 2.3 miles
Surface: Dirt and grass

Contact:
Kevin Kratochvil, Park Ranger
Washington State Parks and Recreation Commission
P.O. Box 106
Gold Bar, WA 98251
206-793-0420

㉙ West Tiger Railroad Grade

Endpoints: West Tiger Mountain Natural Resource Conservation Area
Location: King County
Length: 4 miles
Surface: Original ballast

Contact:
Doug McClelland, Issaquah Unit Forester
Tiger Mountain State Forest
P.O. Box 68
Enumclaw, WA 98022
206-825-1631

㉚ Whatcom County and Bellingham Interurban Trail

Endpoints: Bellingham to Larrabee State Park
Location: Whatcom County
Length: 6.5 miles
Surface: Crushed stone

Contacts:
Roger DeSpain, Director
Whatcom County
Park and Recreation Board
3373 Mount Baker Highway
Bellingham, WA 98226
206-733-2900

Trail Planner
Bellingham Parks
and Recreation Department
210 Lottie Street
Bellingham, WA 98225

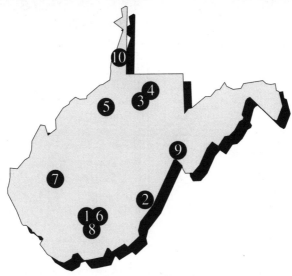

❶ Glade Creek Trail

Endpoints: New River Gorge
National River
Location: Fayette County
Length: 5 miles
Surface: Dirt and gravel

Contact:
Pat Esmond
National Park Service
New River Gorge National River
P.O. Box 246
Glen Jean, WV 25846
304-465-8883

❷ Greenbrier River Trail

Endpoints: North Caldwell to
Cass
Location: Greenbrier and Poca-
hontas Counties
Length: 75 miles
Surface: Crushed stone and
original ballast

Contacts:
Gil Willis, President
Greenbrier River Trail
Association
Highway 219
Slaty Fork, WV 26291
304-572-3771

Danny Talbot
Assistant Superintendent
Watoga State Park
Marlinton, WV 24954
304-799-4087

❸ Harrison County Parks and Recreation Bike and Hike Trail

Endpoints: Clarksburg to Spelter
Location: Harrison County
Length: 6.9 miles
Surface: Original ballast

Contact:
Michael J. Book, Director
Harrison County Parks
and Recreation Commission
301 West Main Street
Clarksburg, WV 26301
304-624-8619

❹ Marion County Trail

Endpoints: Prikets Fort State Park to Fairmont
Location: Marion County
Length: 2 miles
Surface: Packed cinders

Contact:
Ralph S. LaRue, Director
Marion County Parks and
Recreation Commission
P.O. Box 1258
Fairmont, WV 26554
304-363-7037

❺ North Bend State Park Rail-Trail

Endpoints: Wolf Summit to Walker
Location: Harrison, Doddridge, Ritchie and Wood Counties
Length: 20 miles (will be 61 miles when completed)
Surface: Gravel

Contact:
Kevin Kennedy
Superintendent
North Bend State Park
Rail-Trail
Cairo, WV 26337
1-800-call-wva

❻ Southside Junction to Brooklyn Trail

Endpoints: Southside Junction to Brooklyn
Location: New River Gorge National River
Length: 6.4 miles
Surface: Dirt and gravel

Contact:
Pat Esmond
National Park Service
New River Gorge National River
P.O. Box 246
Glen Jean, WV 25846
304-465-8883

7 The Elk River Trail

Endpoints: Coonskin Park
Location: Kanawha County
Length: 1 mile
Surface: Gravel

Contact:
Tom Raker, Director
Kanawha County Parks
and Recreation Commission
2000 Coonskin Drive
Charleston, WV 25311-1087
304-341-8000

8 Thurmond-Minden Trail

Endpoints: Thurmond to
Minden, New River Gorge
National River
Location: Fayette County
Length: 3.2 miles
Surface: Dirt and gravel

Contact:
Pat Esmond
National Park Service
New River Gorge National River
P.O. Box 246
Glen Jean, WV 25846
304-465-8883

9 West Fork Trail

Endpoints: Cheat Junction
to Durbin
Location: Pocahontas County
Length: 26 miles
Surface: Original ballast

Contact:
Jim Thomas, District Ranger
Greenbrier Ranger District
Monongahela National Forest
P.O. Box 67
Bartow, WV 24920
304-456-3335

10 Wheeling Bicycle/ Jogging Path

Endpoints: City of Wheeling
Location: Ohio County
Length: 5 miles
Surface: Asphalt

Contact:
Paul T. McIntire, Sr., Director
Department of Development
City of Wheeling
City-County Building
Wheeling, WV 26003
304-234-3701

WISCONSIN

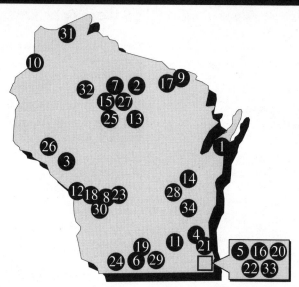

❶ *Ahnapee State Park Trail*

Endpoints: Sturgeon Bay to Algoma
Location: Door and Kewaunee Counties
Length: 15.2 miles
Surface: Crushed stone

 on certain sections

Contact:
Arnie Lindauer
Ahnapee State Park Trail
c/o Potawatomi State Park
3740 Park Drive
Sturgeon Bay, WI 54235
414-746-2890

❷ *Bearskin State Park Trail*

Endpoints: Minocqua to Highway K
Location: Oneida County
Length: 18.4 miles
Surface: Crushed stone

Contact:
Bill Eldred, Superintendent
Bearskin State Park Trail
4125 Highway M
Boulder Junction, WI 54512
715-385-2727

❸ Buffalo River State Park Trail

Endpoints: Fairchild to Mondovi
Location: Eau Claire, Jackson, Trempealeau and Buffalo Counties
Length: 36.4 miles
Surface: Original ballast

Contact:
Philip Palzkill
Perrot State Park
Route 1, Box 407
Trempealeau, WI 54661
608-534-6409

❹ Bugline Trail

Endpoints: Menomonee Falls to Merton
Location: Waukesha County
Length: 13 miles
Surface: Crushed stone

 on certain sections

Contact:
Dave Burch
Senior Landscape Architect
Waukesha County Parks and Planning Commission
500 Riverview Avenue
Waukesha, WI 53188
414-548-7790

❺ Burlington Trail

Endpoints: Burlington to south of Rochester
Location: Racine County
Length: 4 miles
Surface: Crushed stone

Contact:
Tom Statz
Racine County Department of Public Works
14200 Washington Avenue
Sturtevant, WI 53177
414-886-8457

❻ Cheese Country Recreation Trail

Endpoints: Mineral Point to Monroe
Location: Iowa, Lafayette and Green Counties
Length: 47 miles
Surface: Limestone screenings

Contact:
Stephen Hubner
Project Coordinator
Ag Center
Darlington, WI 53530
608-776-4830

⑦ Clover Creek Trail

Endpoints: Chequamegon National Forest, Forest Trail #121 of the Flambeau Trail System, one mile east of Forest Road 148 on Highway 70 to Sailor Lake
Location: Price County
Length: 2.5 miles of 15.8-mile trail is on abandoned rail line
Surface: Dirt and grass

Contact:
Kay Getting
Recreation Planner
1170 4th Ave. South
Park Falls, WI 54552
715-762-2461

⑧ Elroy-Sparta State Park Trail

Endpoints: Elroy to Sparta
Location: Juneau and Monroe Counties
Length: 32 miles
Surface: Crushed stone

Contact:
Ron Nelson, Superintendent
Wildcat Mountain State Park
P.O. Box 99
Ontario, WI 54651
608-337-4775

⑨ Florence County Snowmobile Trail

Endpoints: Nicolet National Forest
Location: Florence County
Length: 4 miles of 32.4-mile system is on abandoned rail line
Surface: Gravel and cinders

Contact:
District Ranger
USFS - Florence Ranger District
Rt. 1, Box 161
Florence, WI 54121
715-528-4464

⑩ Gandy Dancer Trail

Endpoints: Superior to St. Croix Falls (middle portion through Minnesota is not open)
Location: Polk, Burnett and Douglas Counties
Length: 90 miles in three sections
Surface: Original ballast

Burnett County Section

Endpoints: Burnett County line to Minnesota state line
Length: 20 miles

🚜 in winter only

Contact:
Mike Luedeke
Burnett County Forest Administrator
Burnett County Forest and Parks Department
7410 County Highway K
Box 106
Siren, WI 54872
715-349-2157

Polk County Section

Endpoints: St. Croix Falls and Polk County line
Length: 30 miles

Contact:
Bob Wilson
Parks and Recreation Director
Polk County Parks Department
P.O. Box 623
Balsam Lake, WI 54810
715-485-3161

Douglas County Section

Endpoints: Minnesota state line to Superior
Length: 5 miles developed from Minnesota border to Patzau (will be 17 miles when completed)

Contact:
Mark Schroeder
Assistant Parks and Recreation Administrator
Douglas County Forestry Department
P.O. Box 211
Solon Springs, WI 54873
715-378-2219

153

⑪ Glacial Drumlin State Park Trail

Endpoints: Cottage Grove to Waukesha
Location: Waukesha, Jefferson and Dane Counties
Length: 47.2 miles
Surface: Crushed stone

Western Section

Contact:
Dana White
Glacial Drumlin Trail, West
1213 South Main Street
Lake Mills, WI 53551
414-648-8774

Eastern Section

Contact:
Paul Sandgren
Glacial Drumlin Trail, East
N846 W329, C.T.H. "C"
Delafield, WI 53018
414-646-3025

⑫ Great River State Park Trail

Endpoints: Onalaska to Trempealeau National Wildlife Refuge
Location: La Crosse and Trempealeau Counties
Length: 22.5 miles
Surface: Crushed stone

 on certain sections

Contact:
Philip Palzkill
Perrot State Park
Route 1, Box 407
Trempealeau, WI 54661
608-534-6409

⑬ Hiawatha Trail

Endpoints: Tomahawk
Location: Lincoln County
Length: 6.6 miles
Surface: Crushed granite

Contact:
Lincoln County Forestry Land and Parks
Courthouse Building
Merril, WI 54452
715-536-0327

⑭ Hortonville to Oshkosh Recreation Trail

Endpoints: Hortonville to Oshkosh
Location: Outagamie and Winnebago Counties
Length: 20.3 miles
Surface: Crushed stone and original ballast

on certain sections

Outagamie County Section

Contact:
Christopher Brandt, Director
Outagamie County Parks
Route 3, Plamann Park
Appleton, WI 54915
414-733-3019

Winnebago County Section

Contact:
Jeffrey A. Christensen
Parks Director
Winnebago County
Department of Parks
500 East County Road Y
Oshkosh, WI 54901
414-424-0042

⑮ Iodine Snowmobile Trail

Endpoints: Chequamegon National Forest, Trail #104 of the Flambeau Trail System, Wintergreen Parking Lot to Blockhouse Lake Parking Lot
Location: Price County
Length: 2.5 miles of 4-mile trail is on abandoned rail line
Surface: Dirt and grass

Contact:
Kay Getting
Recreation Planner
1170 4th Ave. South
Park Falls, WI 54552
715-762-2461

⑯ Kenosha County Bike Trail

Endpoints: Racine County line to Illinois state line
Location: Kenosha County
Length: 8.2 miles of 14.2-mile trail is on abandoned rail line (6 miles on-street in Kenosha)
Surface: Crushed stone and asphalt

on certain sections

Contact:
Domenick Ventura
or Ric Ladine
Kenosha County Parks
761 Green Bay Road
Kenosha, WI 53144
414-552-8500

17 Kimball Creek Trail

Endpoints: Nicolet National Forest
Location: Forest County
Length: 10 miles of 12-mile trail is on abandoned rail line
Surface: Original ballast

Contact:
District Ranger
USDA - Forest Service
Nicolet National Forest
Eagle River Ranger District
P.O. Box 1809
Eagle River, WI 54521
715-479-2827

18 La Crosse River State Park Trail

Endpoints: Sparta to Medary
Location: Monroe and La Crosse Counties
Length: 21.5 miles
Surface: Crushed stone

Contact:
Ron Nelson, Superintendent
La Crosse River State Park Trail
c/o Wildcat Mountain State Park
P.O. Box 99
Ontario, WI 54651
608-337-4775

19 Military Ridge State Park Trail

Endpoints: Dodgeville to Fitchburg
Location: Iowa and Dane Counties
Length: 37.9 miles developed from Dodgeville to east of Verona (will be 39.6 miles when completed)
Surface: Crushed stone

Contact:
Gregory J. Pittz, Trail Manager
Military Ridge State Park Trail
Route 1, Box 42
Dodgeville, WI 53533
608-935-2315

20 MRK Trail

Endpoints: North of Racine to Seven-Mile Road
Location: Racine County
Length: 5 miles
Surface: Crushed stone

Contact:
Tom Statz
Racine County Department of Public Works
14200 Washington Avenue
Sturtevant, WI 53177
414-886-8457

㉑ New Berlin Trail

Endpoints: East of Waukesha to Milwaukee County line
Location: Waukesha County
Length: 6 miles
Surface: Crushed stone

Contact:
Dave Burch
Senior Landscape Architect
Waukesha County Parks and Planning Commission
500 Riverview Avenue
Waukesha, WI 53188
414-548-7790

㉒ North Shore Trail

Endpoints: South of Racine to Kenosha County line
Location: Racine County
Length: 3 miles
Surface: Crushed stone

Contact:
Tom Statz
Racine County Department of Public Works
14200 Washington Avenue
Sturtevant, WI 53177
414-886-8457

㉓ Omaha Trail

Endpoints: Camp Douglas to Elroy
Location: Juneau County
Length: 12.5 miles
Surface: Asphalt/gravel mix

Contact:
Dale Dorow
Room 16
Courthouse Annex
Mauston, WI 53948
608-847-9389

㉔ Pecatonica State Park Trail

Endpoints: Calamine to Platteville
Location: Lafayette and Grant Counties
Length: 9.6 miles developed from Calamine to Belmont (will be 17 miles when completed)
Surface: Original ballast

Contact:
David Cline
Yellowstone Lake State Park
7896 Lake Road
Blanchardville, WI 53516
608-523-4427

㉕ Pine Line

Endpoints: Medford to Prentice
Location: Taylor and Price
Counties
Length: 26.2 miles
Surface: Gravel and crushed
stone

 on certain sections

in winter only

Contact:
Robert P. Rusch
Secretary, Medford to Prentice
Rail-Trail Association
111 East Division Street
P.O. Box 339
Medford, WI 54451-0339
715-748-2030

㉖ Red Cedar State Trail

Endpoints: Menomonie to
Chippewa River south of
Dunnville
Location: Dunn County
Length: 14.5 miles
Surface: Crushed stone

on certain sections

Contact:
James Janowak
Superintendent
Red Cedar State Trail
Route 6, Box 1
Menomonie, WI 54751
715-232-1242

㉗ Riley Lake Snowmobile Trail

Endpoints: Chequamegon
National Forest, Forest Trail
#120 of the Flambeau Trail
System, one mile south of
highway 70 on Forest Trail 121
to Clifford
Location: Price County
Length: 7.8 miles of 23-mile
trail is on abandoned rail line
Surface: Dirt and grass

Contact:
Kay Getting
Recreation Planner
1170 4th Ave. South
Park Falls, WI 54552
715-762-2461

㉘ Rush Lake Trail

Endpoints: Ripon to Berlin
Location: Fon du Lac,
Winnebago and Green Lake
Counties
Length: 5.3 miles
Surface: Original ballast

Contact:
Jeffrey A. Christensen
Parks Director
Winnebago County
Department of Parks
500 East County Road Y
Oshkosh, WI 54901
414-424-0042

㉙ Sugar River State Park Trail

Endpoints: New Glarus to Brodhead
Location: Green County
Length: 23 miles
Surface: Crushed stone

Contact:
Reynold Zeller, Superintendent
Sugar River State Park Trail
P.O. Box 781
New Glarus, WI 53574
608-527-2334

㉚ The "400" State Trail

Endpoints: Reedsburg to Elroy
Location: Sauk and Juneau Counties
Length: 22 miles
Surface: Crushed limestone with partial parallel original ballast treadway
Will open by the end of 1992

 on certain sections

Contacts:
Ron Nelson, Superintendent
Wildcat Work Unit
P.O. Box 99
Ontario, WI 54651
608-337-4775

Jerry Trumm. Superintendent
Mirror Lake State Park
E10320 Fern Dell Road
Baraboo, WI 53913
608-254-2333

㉛ Tri-County Corridor

Endpoints: Ashland to Superior
Location: Ashland, Bayfield and Douglas Counties
Length: 60 miles
Surface: Original ballast

Contact:
Roy Lindquist
Route 2, Box 48
Iron River, WI 54847
715-372-4580

㉜ Tuscobia State Park Trail

Endpoints: Park Falls to Rice Lake
Location: Price, Sawyer, Washburn and Barron Counties
Length: 74 miles
Surface: Original ballast

 on certain sections

Contact:
Raymond E. Larsen
Superintendent
Tuscobia Trail
P.O. Box 187
Winter, WI 54896
715-634-6513

㉝ Waterford-Wind Lake Trail

Endpoints: Waterford to Wind Lake
Location: Racine County
Length: 5 miles
Surface: Crushed stone

Contact:
Tom Statz
Racine County Department of Public Works
14200 Washington Avenue
Sturtevant, WI 53177
414-886-8457

㉞ Wild Goose State Trail

Endpoints: State Trunk Highway 60 to Fond du Lac
Location: Dodge and Fond du Lac Counties
Length: 29.6 miles
Surface: Crushed limestone (with 3.5-mile parallel dirt treadway between State Trunk Highway 60 and Kindt Street)

Dodge County Section

 in winter only

Contact:
Pamela Kober, Planner
Dodge County Planning and Development Department
Administrative Building
Juneau, WI 53039
414-386-3700

Fond du Lac County Section

Contact:
Sam Tobias
City-County Government Center
160 South Macy Street
Fond du Lac, WI 54935
414-929-3135

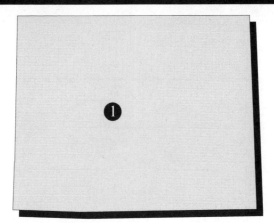

❶ Wyoming Heritage Trail

Endpoints: Riverton to Shoshoni
Location: Fremont County
Length: 22 miles
Surface: Original ballast

Contact:
Mike Morgan
Freemont County Association of Governments
818 South Federal Boulevard
Riverton, WY 82501
307-856-8589

RTC ORDER FORM

YES, I am interested in helping convert abandoned railroad corridors into trails.

I want to become a member of the Rails-to-Trails Conservancy (check dues level):

☐ $18 Individual (NI)   ☐ $50 Patron (NP)

☐ $25 Family (NF)   ☐ $100 Benefactor (NB)

☐ $35 Sustaining (NS)   ☐ Additional Donation (DN)

Send me _____ additional copies of *500 Great Rail-Trails* ($7.95 members; $9.95 non-members)   (GRT) $_____

Send me _____ copies of RTC's *Converting Rails-to-Trails: A Citizen's Manual* ($12 members; $17 non-members)   (CM) $ _____

_____ Please send me a **free** copy of RTC's *Fact Sheets and Studies*, a list of 29 publications relating to all facets of rail-trail conversion.

Shipping and Handling $3.50

TOTAL: $_____

To order by Mastercard or Visa only, use our easy toll-free number by calling: 1-800-888-7747, ext. 11

Or send a check payable to Rails-to-Trails Conservancy to: Rails-to-Trails Conservancy, Shipping Department, P.O. Box 295, Federalsburg, MD 21632-0295.

Name _____

Address _____

City, State, Zip _____

Phone (day) _____

(evening) _____

Rails-to-Trails Conservancy is a non-profit, charitable organization as qualified under Section 501(c)(3) of the Internal Revenue Code. Contributions are tax-exempt to the extent permitted by law.

GRT